THE ART

OF

SAIL-MAKING,

AS PRACTISED IN

The Royal Navy,

AND

ACCORDING TO THE MOST APPROVED METHODS

IN THE

MERCHANT SERVICE,

ACCOMPANIED WITH THE

PARLIAMENTARY REGULATIONS RELATIVE TO SAILS AND SAIL-CLOTH;

The Admiralty Instructions for

MANUFACTURING CANVAS FOR HER MAJESTY'S NAVY,

Form of Tender, &c.

ILLUSTRATED BY

NUMEROUS FIGURES, WITH FULL AND ACCURATE TABLES.

THE FOURTH EDITION,
CORRECTED AND IMPROVED.

===

LONDON:

PRINTED FOR CHARLES WILSON,

(Late J. W. Norie and Wilson,)

CHARTSELLER TO THE ADMIRALTY, THE HON. EAST INDIA COMPANY,
AND CORPORATION OF TRINITY HOUSE,

At the Navigation Warehouse and Naval Academy,
No. 157, LEADENHALL STREET.

1843.

Entered at Stationers' Hall.

J. Dennett, Printer, 121, Fleet Street.

This scarce antiquarian book is included in our special *Legacy Reprint Series*. In the interest of creating a more extensive selection of rare historical book reprints, we have chosen to reproduce this title even though it may possibly have occasional imperfections such as missing and blurred pages, missing text, poor pictures, markings, dark backgrounds and other reproduction issues beyond our control. Because this work is culturally important, we have made it available as a part of our commitment to protecting, preserving and promoting the world's literature. Thank you for your understanding.

REPRESENTATION of a SAIL LOFT.

London. Published as the Act directs, January 11th 1843, by Charles Wilson, late Norie & Wilson, at the Navigation Warehouse, No. 157, Leadenhall Street.

PREFACE.

The following Treatise on Sail-making was first published in "THE ELEMENTS AND PRACTICE OF RIGGING, SEAMANSHIP, NAVAL TACTICS," &c. &c. a work in two volumes quarto.

As an object of particular convenience and advantage to *Naval Artists*, the then proprietor had been solicited to separate the arts there treated of, and to publish them in a smaller form. In compliance with this request, the work was re-published in four volumes octavo, with a separate volume of plates.

The first edition of the ART OF SAIL-MAKING was produced in the present form, and met with a favourable reception, from the merits of its correct delineation and clear description; by these its utility was felt, and its value justly appreciated of greater import. The patronage bestowed on the first edition called for a second and a third, in which a new set of Tables was introduced.

The copyright of the work having fallen into the hands of the present proprietor at a period when all the impressions of the third edition were disposed of, he has been induced, by the very favourable reception the three former have experienced, to print a fourth edition, for which he has employed the best abilities in renewing the designs of the sails, and the best efforts of printing to embellish the whole; the entire of the sheets have been carefully revised, and the set of Tables introduced in the last edition has undergone a strict examination; to which have been added the Admiralty Instructions for manufacturing of Sail-cloth for Her Majesty's Navy, Form of Tender for Canvas, &c.

In issuing the present edition to the public, the proprietor trusts that the pains bestowed on it, will guarantee a continuance of the patronage the three former editions have met with; and that to the experienced Sail-maker or his Assistant, it will be found useful as a book of reference, and to the less experienced and uninformed an ample fund of instruction.

Navigation Warehouse and Naval Academy,
157, Leadenhall Street, Jan. 11, 1843.

CONTENTS.

	Page
ALPHABETICAL EXPLANATION OF THE TECHNICAL TERMS RELATIVE TO SAILS, AND DESCRIPTION OF THE TOOLS USED IN SAIL-MAKING	1
DESCRIPTION AND USE OF SAILS	10
The sails of a ship	11
The sails of two-mast vessels	ib.
The sails of one-mast vessels	ib.
Boats' sails	12
Names of the different parts of sails	ib.
Extending sails to the yard, &c.	ib.
Tanning of sails	14
GENERAL RULES AND INSTRUCTIONS FOR SAIL-MAKING	15
Cutting out sails	ib.
Seams	17
Tablings of sails	18
Linings of sails	19
Holes in sails	ib.
Bolt-rope	20
A Table of the number of yarns in each strand of bolt-ropes, and the threads for sewing them on	21
A Table of the circumference of bolt-rope for sails of ships, sloops, brigs, cutters, and boats	22
Clues of sails	24
Cringles of sails	26
Bonnet and drabler of sails	27
Reef-hanks	ib.
Proposed improvements in sail-making	28
RULES FOR ASCERTAINING THE QUANTITY OF CANVAS CONTAINED IN THE DIFFERENT SAILS	30
A TABLE OF THE NUMBER OF REEFS, POINTS, ROPE-BANDS, AND GASKETS, USED IN THE FITTING OF SAILS	38

CONTENTS.

PARTICULAR DIRECTIONS FOR MAKING EVERY SAIL, EACH ILLUSTRATED WITH A FIGURE, VIZ.

	Page
A ship's main-course	39
——— fore-course	41
——— mizen-course	43
——— storm-mizen	104
——— main-top-sail	44
——— fore-top-sail	46
——— mizen-top-sail	48
——— main-top-gallant-sail	49
——— fore-top-gallant-sail	50
——— mizen-top-gallant-sail	51
——— main-royal-sail	52
——— fore-royal-sail	53
——— mizen-royal-sail	ib.
——— sky-scrapers	103
——— main-stay-sail	54
——— fore-stay-sail	55
——— mizen-stay-sail	56
——— main-top-mast-stay-sail	58
——— fore-top-mast-stay-sail	59
——— middle-stay-sail	61
——— mizen-top-mast-stay-sail	62
——— main-top-gallant-stay-sail	63
——— royal-stay-sails	104
——— lower-main-studding-sails	65
——— lower-fore-studding-sails	66
——— main-top-mast-studding-sails	67
——— fore-top-mast-studding-sails	68
——— main-top-gallant-studding-sails	69
——— fore-top-gallant-studding-sails	70
——— jib	71
——— sprit-sail-course	73
——— sprit-sail-top-sail	74
——— sprit-sail-top-gallant-sail	104
——— driver-boom-sail	75
A brig's main-sail	77
A cutter's main-sail	79
——— try-sail, or storm main-sail	81
A sloop's main-sail	83
——— try-sail or storm-main-sail	85

CONTENTS.

	Page
A sloop's square-sail or cross-jack	87
——— top-sail	88
——— save-all top-sail	89
——— gaff-top-sail	90
——— top-gallant-sail	91
——— water-sail	92
——— fore-sail	93
——— jib	94
——— storm-jib	96
——— flying-jib	97
——— ring-tail-sail	98
A smack's main-sail	99
——— fore-sail	101
——— jib	102
Wing-sail for ketches	104
A boat's settee-sail	105
——— latteen-sail	106
——— sliding gunter-sail	107
——— shoulder-of-mutton-sail	108
——— lug-sail	109
——— main-sprit-sail	110
——— fore-sprit-sail	111
——— mizen-sprit-sail	112
——— fore-sail	113
——— jib	ib.
Mast-coats	114
Rudder-coats	115
Wind-sail or ventilator	116
Quarter-cloths	117
Awnings	119
A smoke-sail	121
TABLES of the DIMENSIONS of ALL SAILS, and the QUANTITIES of CANVAS contained in every part of each sail, with the SORTS of CANVAS of which they are respectively made, for ships of all rates, viz.	
Ships of 100 guns, or 2164 tons	124
——— 90 guns, or 1870 tons	125
——— 80 guns, or 1920 tons	126
——— 74 guns, or 1800 tons	127
——— 64 guns, or 1569 tons	128
——— 50 guns, or 1444 tons	129

viii   CONTENTS.

	Page
A ship of 60 guns, or 1500 tons	130
——— 46 guns, or 1200 tons	131
——— 36 guns, or 900 tons	132
——— 32 guns, or 680 tons	133
——— 28 guns, or 600 tons	134
——— 24 guns, or 520 tons	135
——— 20 guns, or 430 tons	136
Sloop of 422 tons	137
——— 361 tons	138
Brigs of 14 guns, or 200 tons	139
Cutters of 14 guns, or 200 tons	140
Boats of about 6 tons	ib.
NUMBER of SAILS in a SUIT for eight months' service in the ROYAL NAVY	141
The QUALITY of CANVAS of which the different sails are made in the MERCHANT-SERVICE, viz.	
Sails made of canvas No. 1, in the merchant-service	141
——————— No. 2, ———————	ib.
——————— No. 3, ———————	ib.
——————— No. 4, ———————	ib.
——————— No. 5, ———————	ib.
——————— No. 6, ———————	ib.
——————— No. 7, ———————	ib.
——————— No. 8, ———————	ib.
A TABLE of the QUANTITY of CANVAS and OTHER MATERIALS, used in making a suit of sails for eight months' service in the royal navy; and a single suit for East and West India ships	142
PARLIAMENTARY REGULATIONS relative to sails and sail-cloth.	143
DUTIES payable upon the IMPORTATION of sail-cloth and sails.	151
ADMIRALTY INSTRUCTIONS for manufacturing CANVAS for Her Majesty's Navy	152
FORM of TENDER for CANVAS for Her Majesty's Navy	155
CONDITIONS	156
DECLARATION to accompany the TENDER	158

THE ART OF SAIL-MAKING.

EXPLANATION OF THE TECHNICAL TERMS RELATIVE TO SAILS,

AND

DESCRIPTION OF THE TOOLS USED IN SAIL-MAKING.

AWNING. A screen of canvas, to be expanded over the decks, for protecting them and the crew from the heat of the sun.

BAG-REEF. A fourth or lower reef, sometimes used in the royal navy.

BALANCE-REEF. A reef-band that crosses a sail diagonally, and is used to contract it in a storm.

BANDS. Pieces of canvas, from one-sixth to a whole breadth, strongly sewed across the sail to strengthen it.

To BEND a Sail. To affix it to its proper yard, mast, or stay.

BOLT-ROPE. The rope sewed on the edges of sails to prevent their rending. The bolt-rope on the perpendicular or sloping edges is called the leech-rope; that at the bottom, the foot-rope; and that on the top of the sail, the head-rope.

BONNET. An additional part of a sail, made to fasten with latchings to the foot of the sails of some vessels with one mast, in moderate winds. It is exactly similar to the foot of the sail it is intended for.

BOWLINE. A rope attached by the bridles to the bowline cringles, on the leech of top-sails and other square sails, to keep tight the windward or weather leech of the sail, when on a wind.

BRAILS. Ropes to draw up the foot, lower corner, and the skirts, of mizen-courses, and other large fore and aft sails for furling, or when tacking.

BRIDLES of the bowline. Short ropes, or legs, fastened to the bowline cringles on the leeches of sails.

BUNT. The middle part of the foot of square sails, and the foremost leech of stay-sails cut with a nock.

BUNTLINE. A rope fastened to the buntline cringles, on the foot of square sails, to draw them up to their yards.

BUNTLINE CLOTH. The lining sewed up the sail, in the direction of the buntline, to prevent the sail's being chafed.

CANVAS. For the royal navy, canvas or sail-cloth is 24 inches wide; and 38 yards are called a bolt. To distinguish the different qualities, each bolt is numbered, and should weigh as follows: No. 1, 44lb.; No. 2, 41; No. 3, 38; No. 4, 35; No. 5, 32; No. 6, 29; No. 7, 24; and No. 8, 21 pounds: from No. 1 to 6 is termed double, and above No. 6, single, canvas.

CLUE. The lower corner of a sail, where the clue-rope is spliced, and the sheet fastened.

CLUE-ROPE. A short rope, larger than the bolt-rope on the sail, into which it is spliced, at the lower corners of square sails, and the after corners of stay-sails and boom-sails. It is there formed into a loop, to which the sheets are fastened.

COURSES. The main-sail, fore-sail, sprit-sail, and mizen of ships.

CRINGLES. Small holes formed on the bolt-ropes of sails by intertwisting the strand of a rope alternately round itself and through the strands of the bolt-rope, till it assumes the shape of a ring. To the cringles the end of a rope is fastened, to haul the sail up to the yard, &c.

DRABLER. An additional part of a sail, laced to the bottom of the bonnet of a square sail, in Dutch sloops, &c.

DRIVER. See SPANKER.

DROP of a sail. A term sometimes used to courses and top-sails instead of depth.

EARINGS. The upper part of the leech-rope, worked into the shape of a cringle; and used to extend the upper corners of sails to their yards or gaffs, with small ropes also called earings.

TOOLS AND TERMS USED IN SAIL-MAKING.

FID. A round tapering pin, made of hard wood, to thrust between the strands of a rope, and make a hole to admit the strand of another rope, in splicing.

To FURL. To roll a sail close to the yard, and thus making it fast.

GASKET. A plaited cord used to fasten the folded parts of a sail to the yard, when furling or reefing.

GOOSEWINGS of a sail. The clues, or lower corners of a ship's main-sail or fore-sail.

GORES. Angles cut slopewise at one or both ends of such cloths as widen or increase the depth of a sail.

GROMMET. A small wreath made by intertwisting together the ends of a short piece of rope or line.

HALIARDS. The ropes or tackle employed to hoist the yards or sails.

HANKS. A sort of wooden rings, formed by the bending of a piece of tough wood, which are confined to the stays by notches cut in the ends.

HEAD-SAILS. All the sails belonging to the fore-mast and bowsprit.

HEADSTICK. A short round stick, with a hole in each end strongly sewed to the end of some triangular fore-sails and jibs, to prevent the head of the sail from twisting; the head-rope is thrust through the holes before it is sewed on the sail.

HEAVING-MALLET. A mallet with a small cylindrical head, used as a lever to strain tight the cross stitches and beat them close, when sewing on the bolt-rope.

HOIST. The foremost leeches of stay-sails and mast leech of boom-sails.

HOLES in sails are made with an instrument called a stabber, or a pegging-awl. In most sails the holes are cut with a knife, and are fenced round by stitching the edge to a small grommet: such are the holes on the head of a sail for the ropebands or lacing of square sails, and for seizings on sails that bend to hoops and hanks. Holes are likewise made across the sail in the reef-bands; at the clues, for marling on the clue-rope; and at the top brims of top-sails, for marling on the foot-rope. Holes, when finished, should be stretched up with a fid or marling-spike.

HOUSE-LINE. Small lines of three threads. This line is also

called marling-line, used to marl the clue-rope at the clues, and to seize the corners of sails.

JIB. A sail set on the jib-boom of ships, and on the bowsprit of sloops, cutters, &c.

LACEING. The rope or line used to confine the heads of sails to their yards or gaffs.

LASHING. A short rope used to confine one object to another, by several turns round it, and securing the end.

LATCHINGS. Loops formed on the line that is sewed to the head of a bonnet to connect it with the foot of a sail.

LATEEN-SAIL. A triangular sail, bent at the foremast leech to a yard that hoists obliquely to the mast, and is connected with it, at one-third the length of the yard.

LEECHES, or skirts. The perpendicular or sloping edges of sails.

LININGS. The canvas sewed on the leeches and middle of a sail to strengthen it.

MARLING. Securing clue-ropes to the clues of sails, by passing a line round the rope and through each marling-hole with a hitch knot.

MARLING-SPIKE. A tapered iron pin, either with or without a short wooden handle, bent towards the point. It is used to open the strands of a rope for splicing, and to strain tight the seizing of clues, &c.

MAST-CLOTH. The lining in the middle on the aft side of top-sails, to prevent the sail's being chafed by the mast.

NEEDLES have three sides towards the point, and are of various sizes. They bear the following names, viz. large marline, small marline, double bolt-rope, large bolt-rope, small bolt-rope, store, old work, tabling, and flat-seam, needles. The needles should be no longer than is necessary to carry the twine, and the edges should be taken off, that the canvas may not be cut.

NOCK. The foremost upper corner of boom-sails, and of stay-sails cut with a square tack.

PALM. A flat round piece of iron, used instead of a thimble, and checquered in the middle, to hinder the head of the needle from slipping. It is sewed on a piece of leather or canvas, having a hole for the thumb to go through, which encircles the hand so that the iron, when used, is against the palm.

TOOLS AND TERMS USED IN SAIL-MAKING.

PARCELLING is encircling a rope, after it is wormed, with narrow pieces of old canvas, well tarred, to make a fair surface for the serving.

PEEK. The upper corner of triangular sails, and upper outer corner of fore and aft sails.

PEGGING-AWL. An instrument for making holes with, now called a Stabber, which see. It has four sharp edges towards the point, and is smaller than a stabber.

POINTS. Short pieces of flat plaited cordage, tapering from the middle to the ends, used to reef the square sails.

PRICKER. A small instrument, like a marling-spike, but straight, to make the holes with.

REEF. The portion of sail contained between the reef-bands and nearest edge of the sail, at head or foot.

REEF-BANDS. The bands in which the reef-holes are made when sewed across the sail.

REEF-HANKS. Short pieces of log-line, or other small line, sewed at certain distances on the reefs of boom-sails.

REEF-TACKLE PENDENT. A rope employed to hoist the reef of a topsail to the yard, to reef the sail.

REELS FOR TWINE are short cylindrical pieces of wood, having the sides hollowed, and a hole bored through the middle.

A BENCH-REEL is similar to a spinning-wheel, and is used to expedite winding the twine from the skains to the twine-reel. This instrument is here drawn left-handed; it should be completely reversed.

6   TOOLS AND TERMS USED IN SAIL-MAKING.

A YARN-REEL is a circular board, nailed in the middle to a piece of oak, four inches square and sixteen inches long, and is used to wind spun-yarn on; through the centre is bored a hole, by which it turns round a bolt, as on an axis.

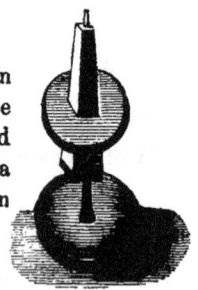

RING-TAIL-SAIL. A small sail, extended by a small mast and a boom, over the stern. A boat's main-sail is generally made to answer both purposes.

ROACH-LEECH. A term signifying the curve on the mast-leech of some fore and aft sails, &c.

ROPE-BANDS. Short pieces of plaited cordage, used to fasten the head of a sail to its yard.

ROYALS. Sails to set on their respective masts, above the top-gallant-sails.

RUBBER. A small iron instrument, in a wooden handle, to rub down or flatten the seams. The iron ends of rubbers are now made square.

SAIL-HOOK. A small iron hook, with an eye in one end, to which a cord is spliced: it is used to confine the work, while sewing, by hooking on the canvas, the cord being fastened to some convenient place.

SEAMS. The two edges of canvas where laid over each other and sewed down.

SEIZING. Joining one part of a rope to another with several round and cross-turns of small cord or line.

SELVAGE. The edges of cloth as finished in weaving.

SERVING, is winding small line or spunyarn tightly round a rope by a mallet, to preserve it from wet, &c. The line or spun-yarn being wound up in a ball, two or more turns are taken from it round the rope, confining the end under the turns: the mallet is then placed on the rope, and two or more yarns are passed round the rope and mallet, and round the handle, then, turning the mallet (whilst another person passes the ball round the rope), it leaves the spunyarn on the rope, and draws it tight.

SERVING-MALLET. A wooden instrument, composed of a short cylindrical head, with a handle through its centre. Along the upper surface of the head is cut a circular groove, to fit the convexity of the rope.

SERVING-BOARD. A small piece of board, seven or eight inches long and three inches broad, tapering to one end as a handle. It has a small notch or groove cut in the middle of the broad end, and one or two on the sides, in which the spunyarn is twisted. Its use is the same as the mallet, but for small rope only.

SHEET. A rope to spread the foot of a sail, attached to the clues of square sails, and the after clue of other sails, except studding-sails: on them it is fastened to the inner clue.

SHOULDER-OF-MUTTON-SAIL is triangular, similar to the lateen-sail, but is attached to a mast instead of a yard.

SLACK-CLOTH. A certain quantity of cloth allowed to be gradually gathered up, in sewing on the bolt-rope to the sail, more than the length of bolt-rope; otherwise the rope, by stretching in the wearing, might occasion the sail to split.

SLIDING-GUNTER-SAIL. A triangular sail, used in boats, bent at its foremost leech to hoops or grommets that slide on the lower mast; the peak or head is attached to a small topmast, that slides up, in the direction of the lower mast, through two hoops fixed, at its head, about three feet asunder. When the topmast is lowered, the sails furl close up to the lower mast.

SPLICE. Two ends of a rope joined neatly together, by opening the strands and placing them equally in each other, and thrusting the ends through the intervals of the opposite strands alternately, the opening being previously made with a fid or marlingspike.

SPUNYARN. Three or four yarns of half-worn rope, tarred and twisted together by a winch or whirls.

STABBER. An instrument similar to a pricker, only being triangular instead of square.

STAY. A large rope employed to sustain the mast, by extending from its upper part towards the fore part of the ship, where it is securely fastened, and on which the stay-sails are set.

STAY-HOLES. Holes made through stay-sails, at certain distances along the hoist, through which they are seized to the hanks on the stay.

STUCK. The term used for being stitched.

TABLING. A broad hem made on the skirts of sails, by turning the edge over and sewing it down. It is to strengthen the sail for sewing on the bolt-rope.

TABLED. The edges turned over and sewed down.

TACK. A rope used to confine the clues of the main-sail and fore-sail forward occasionally in a fixed position, and also to confine the foremost lower corners of stay-sails, boom-sails, and fore-sails of sloops; and the outer lower corners of studding-sails.

TACK OF A SAIL. That place to which the tack is fastened.

THIMBLE. An iron ring, having a groove formed in its outer circumference. Thimbles are fixed in the cringles of sails where iron hooks are used, as the hook of a tackle, &c.

THUMB-STALL. A ferrule, made of iron, horn, or leather, with the edges turned up to receive the thread, in sewing. It is worn on the thumb, to tighten the stitches.

TOP-BRIM (in the royal navy), a space in the middle of the foot of a top-sail, containing one-fifth of the number of its cloths. It is so called from its situation, being near the fore part of the top, or platform on the mast, when the sail is extended.

TOP-LINING. The lining sewed to the aft-side of top-sails, to preserve the sail from chafing of the top.

TOP-SAILS. Sails which are set upon the respective top-masts.

TOP-GALLANT-SAILS. Sails which are set above the top-sails, upon their respective masts.

TRY-SAIL. A small sail used by brigs and cutters in blowing weather.

TWINE is of two sorts, extra and ordinary; the extra is for seaming, and runs 360 fathoms to the pound; the ordinary is used to sew on the bolt-rope, and runs 200 fathoms to the pound. Twine for the navy is of three threads.

WATER-SAIL. A sail set under any boom-sail.

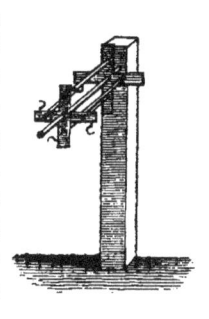

WINCH, to make or twist spunyarn with, is made of eight spokes, four at each end, and four wooden pins, fifteen inches long, driven through the end of them. Through the centre of the spokes is bored a hole for an iron bolt to pass through, that serves for an axis. The motion is given to the winch by the hand; on the edges of the spokes is a small hook to stop the yarn when twisting, after which the spunyarn is wound round the body of the winch.

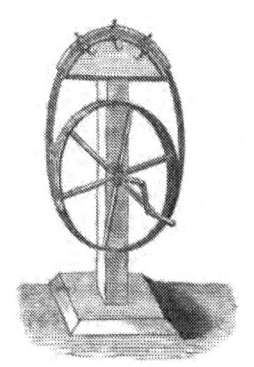

WHIRLS. Short wires with a hook at one end, going through a hole in a cylindrical piece of wood; the wood in which they turn is hollowed on the outside to receive a strap of canvas or leather: three of these whirls are retained by notches cut on the edge of a semicircular rib of wood hollowed on the back, three inches square, and ten inches long, fastened against an upright fixed by a tenon into a large block of wood: a spoke-wheel, about three feet diameter, turns on a large pin, or axis, driven into the middle of the upright; and round this wheel and the woods of the whirls passes a tight canvas or leather strap; so that turning the spoke-wheel puts the whirls in motion, and the yarns, being hung to the hooks, are twisted together.

WORMING is winding small lines or spunyarn along the contline of a rope, to produce a fair surface for serving.

DESCRIPTION AND USE OF SAILS.

SAILS are made of canvas, of different textures, and are extended on or between the masts, to receive the wind, and force the vessel through the water. They are quadrilateral or triangular; and are skirted round with bolt-ropes, as hereafter described.

All sails derive their names from the mast, yard, boom, or stay, to or upon which they are extended or attached: thus, the principal sail, extended upon the main-mast, is called the main-sail, or main-course; that upon the main-top-mast is termed the main-top-sail; that upon the main-top-gallant-mast is named the main-top-gallant-sail; and the main-top-gallant-royal is so called from its being spread across the upper part of the main-top-gallant-mast. The fore-sail or fore-course is so denominated from the fore-mast; the fore-top-sail from the fore-top-mast; the fore-top-gallant-sail from the fore-top-gallant-mast; and the fore-top-gallant-royal from being spread on the upper part of the fore-top-gallant-mast; the mizen-course from the mizen-mast; the driver-boom-sail from the driver-boom; the spanker from the spanker-boom; the mizen-top-sail from the mizen-top-mast; the mizen-top-gallant-sail from the mizen-top-gallant-mast; and the mizen-top-gallant-royal from its being spread on the upper part of the mizen-top-gallant-mast. The stay-sails are denominated from the stays on which they are respectively hoisted.

The studding-sails, being extended beyond the different yards of the main and fore-masts, are likewise named, according to their stations, the lower studding-sail, the top-mast-studding-sail, and the top-gallant-studding-sail.

THE SAILS OF A SHIP,

Or vessel of three masts, are the courses or lower sails; driver or spanker; fore, main, mizen, and sprit sail, top-sails, next above their respective courses; fore, main, and mizen, top-gallant-sails, next above the top-sails; and the royals above them: studding-sails are set beyond the leeches of the main and fore courses, top-sails, and top-gallant-sails; and between the masts, bowsprit, and jib-boom, upon the stays, are the jib and stay-sails.

The courses are the main-sail, fore-sail, mizen and sprit-sail; which are, except the mizen, fixed on their respective yards at right angles with the ship's length; the mizen is bent to a yard or gaff parallel with the ship's length. The stay-sails between the main and mizen-masts are, the mizen-stay-sail, the mizen-top-mast-stay-sail, and sometimes a mizen-top-gallant-stay-sail above the latter: those between the main and fore-masts are the main-stay-sail, main-top-mast-stay-sail, middle stay-sail, and main-top-gallant-stay-sail: those between the fore-mast and the bowsprit are, the fore-stay-sail, the fore-top-mast-stay-sail, and jib. Many ships have two jibs.

THE SAILS OF TWO-MAST VESSELS

Are, in a snow, similar to those on the fore and main-masts of a ship, except the sail called a try-sail, used instead of a mizen, which it resembles; it is extended towards the stern, and is fastened by hoops round a small mast, called a try-sail-mast, fixed near the aftside of the main-mast in a block of wood in the quarter-deck, at the foot, and attached to the main-top at the head.

The sails of a brig are also similar to those on the main and fore-masts of a ship, excepting the main-sail, which is set in the plane of her keel, and is extended by a gaff at the head and a boom at the foot; the foremost leech being fastened by hoops round the main-mast.

The sails of a schooner are like those of a sloop on the fore-mast, and like those of a brig on the main-mast.

THE SAILS OF ONE-MAST VESSELS.

Sloops, cutters, smacks, hoys, &c. have a main-sail abaft the mast, as the brigs; upon and before the mast they have a square sail, or cross-jack; and, above the cross-jack, a small sail, called a save-all top-sail; above that is a top-sail, called a swallow-tailed top-sail, and the next is the top-gallant-sail. Some large sloops have a royal above the top-gallant-sail, and studding sails beyond the leeches of the square sail. Before the mast is a fore-sail, a jib, and a flying-jib. Abaft the after-leech of the main-sail, in calm weather, is hoisted a ringtail-sail; over the head of the main-sail a gaff-top-sail; over the stern, under the boom, a water-sail; and some have try-sails.

There is an additional part of a sail, called a BONNET; it is laced at the bottom, or foot, of the fore-sail, try-sail, and storm main-sails, of some vessels with one mast, in moderate winds. It is made like the foot of the sail it is intended for, and has latchings in the upper part, to correspond with and go through holes in the foot of the sail by which it is fastened.

BOATS' SAILS.

Some have a main-sail, fore-sail, and jib, as in sloops; others have lug-sails. Some have sprit-sails, and lateen or settee sails, according to their various uses, the fancy of the owners, or the country to which they belong.

NAMES OF THE DIFFERENT PARTS OF SAILS.

In quadrilateral sails, the upper edge is called the head: the sides or skirts are called leeches: and the lower edge is named the foot. If the head is parallel with the foot, the two lower corners are called clues, and the upper corners earings.

In triangular sails, and in quadrilateral ones where the head is not parallel to the foot, the foremost corner at the foot is called the tack; the after lower corner, the clue; the upper inner corner, the nock; and the upper outer corner, the peek; the foremost perpendicular, or goring edge, the fore-leech; and the hindmost, the after-leech.

EXTENDING SAILS TO THE YARD, &c.

Quadrilateral sails are extended by yards, as the principal sails; by yards and booms, as studding-sails; a gaff, as mizen-courses; or by a boom and gaff, as drivers and spankers, or boom-main-sails, of brigs, sloops, &c.

Triangular sails are spread by a stay, as the jib and stay sails; or by a mast, and sometimes by a yard, acting as a kind of gaff, as lateen or shoulder-of-mutton sails; the foremost leech, or edge, is attached to the yard, mast, or stay, the whole length.

The heads of quadrilateral sails, and the fore leeches or head of triangular sails, are attached to their yards, or gaffs, by a number of small cords, called rope-bands, or by a line, called the lacing.

The heads of quadrilateral sails, when not parallel to the foot, lace to the yard or gaff by a line, reeved spirally through each hole in the head, and round the yard or gaff. The nock and peek are lashed by the earings.

The fore-leech of mizen courses, drivers, and spankers, and fore and aft main-sails, lace to the mast by a line, reeved through the holes in the leech, backwards and forwards, on the foreside of the mast, or to hoops round the mast.

Stay-sails are extended upon the stays, between the masts, with hanks or grommets, and are drawn up and down as a curtain slides upon its rod; their lower parts are stretched out by a tack and sheet.

The lower corners of main-sails and fore-sails of ships are extended by a tack and a sheet; the foremost lower corners of fore and aft sails by a tack, and the after lower corners by a sheet.

The clues of a top-sail are drawn out to the extremities of the lower yard by two large ropes, called the top-sail sheets; the clues of the top-gallant-sails are extended upon the top-sail yard-arms by the top-gallant sheets; and the clues of the royal-sails are lashed to the top-gallant yard-arms.

Studding sails are set beyond the skirts or leeches of the main-sail, fore-sail, top-sail, and top-gallant-sail, of ships, snows, brigs, &c. Their upper edges, or heads, are extended by yards; their lower ones, by booms run out beyond the extremities of the yards. These sails are set in favourable winds and moderate weather, or in chasing.

The ropes, by which the lower yards and sails are hoisted to their proper heights on the mast, are called the jears. The ropes employed for this purpose, to all other sails, are called haliards.

The principal sails are expanded by haliards, sheets, and bowlines; and the courses are always stretched out below by a tack and sheet: they are drawn or trussed up together by bunt-lines, clue-garnets, or clue-lines, leech-lines, reef-tackles, slab-lines, spilling-lines, and brails.

The courses, top-sails, and top-gallant-sails, are wheeled about the mast, to suit the various directions of the wind, by braces: the higher studding-sails, and, in general, all the stay and boom sails, are drawn down, to be furled or reefed, by down-haulers.

TANNING OF SAILS.

The sails of fishing-vessels are generally tanned;* lightermen, &c. use the following composition to colour and preserve their sails, viz. horse grease and tar, mixed to a proper consistence, and coloured with red or yellow ochre, with which, when heated, the sails are payed over.

The following method is also much approved, viz. the sail, being spread on the grass, is made thoroughly wet with sea-water, and then payed over, on both sides, with brown or red ochre mixed with sea-water to the consistence of cream; it is then well rubbed over on both sides with linseed-oil. The sail may be used within twenty-four hours after being oiled.

The tanning of sails in the royal navy has been tried, but is not approved of.

It is advisable, before any new sail is bent, to soak it in salt-water for some time, which prevents the sail, in a great measure, from mildewing.

* That is, a quantity of oak-bark is boiled, in the liquor of which the sail is immerged, if it be not too large; and when it is, the boiling liquor is used with a mop, and payed over the sail, with red ochre, or not, according to opinion.

GENERAL RULES AND INSTRUCTIONS FOR SAIL-MAKING.

CUTTING OUT SAILS.

SAILS are cut out cloth by cloth, the width being governed by the length of the yard, gaff, boom, or stay; the depth by the height of the mast. The width and depth being given, find the number of cloths the width requires, allowing for seams, tabling on the leeches and slack cloth; and in the depth allow for tabling on the head and foot. For sails cut square on the head and foot, with gores only on the leeches, as some top-sails, &c. the cloths on the head between the leeches are cut square to the depth; and the gores on the leeches are found by dividing the depth of the sail by the number of cloths gored, which gives the length of each gore. The gore is set down from a square with the opposite selvage, and, the canvas being cut diagonally, the longest-gored side of one cloth makes the shortest side of the next; consequently, the first gore being known, the rest are cut by it.

For the length of gores corresponding to the depth on the selvage, observe the Table on the following page.

TABLE

Shewing the Length of any Gore by its Depth, from 1 Inch to 6 Feet in Depth, on the Selvage of Canvas 24 Inches wide.

EXAMPLE.

In the Column of Depth, find the Depth given, and the opposite Column will shew the proper Length. Suppose the Depth be 3 Feet 5 Inches, opposite to it will be found 4 Feet, which is the Length required.

Depth down the Selvage.		Length of the Gore.		Depth down the Selvage.		Length of the Gore.		Depth down the Selvage.		Length of the Gore.	
Feet	Inch.	Feet	Inch.	Feet	Inch.	Feet	Inch.	Feet	Inch.	Feet	Inch.
0	1	2	0	2	1	2	10¾	4	1	4	7
0	2	2	0	2	2	2	11½	4	2	4	7⅞
0	3	2	0⅛	2	3	3	0¼	4	3	4	8¾
0	4	2	0¼	2	4	3	1	4	4	4	9⅝
0	5	2	0⅜	2	5	3	1¾	4	5	4	10½
0	6	2	0½	2	6	3	2½	4	6	4	11⅜
0	7	2	0¾	2	7	3	3¼	4	7	5	0¼
0	8	2	1⅛	2	8	3	4⅛	4	8	5	1⅛
0	9	2	1½	2	9	3	5	4	9	5	2
0	10	2	1⅞	2	10	3	5⅞	4	10	5	2⅞
0	11	2	2¼	2	11	3	6¾	4	11	5	3¾
1	0	2	2¾	3	0	3	7⅝	5	0	5	4⅝
1	1	2	3¼	3	1	3	8½	5	1	5	5½
1	2	2	3¾	3	2	3	9⅜	5	2	5	6⅜
1	3	2	4¼	3	3	3	10¼	5	3	5	7¼
1	4	2	4¾	3	4	3	11⅛	5	4	5	8⅛
1	5	2	5¼	3	5	4	0	5	5	5	9
1	6	2	5¾	3	6	4	0⅞	5	6	5	10
1	7	2	6¼	3	7	4	1¾	5	7	5	11
1	8	2	7	3	8	4	2⅝	5	8	6	0
1	9	2	7¾	3	9	4	3½	5	9	6	1
1	10	2	8½	3	10	4	4⅜	5	10	6	2
1	11	2	9¼	3	11	4	5¼	5	11	6	3
2	0	2	10	4	0	4	6⅛	6	0	6	4

In the LEECHES OF TOP-SAILS CUT HOLLOW, such as the fore-top-sails of north country colliers in general, the upper gores are longer than the lower ones; and, in sails cut with a roach leech, the lower gores are longer than the upper ones. This must be regulated by judgment, and care taken that the whole of the gores do not exceed the depth of the leech. By drawing on paper the gored side of the sail, and delineating the breadth of every cloth by a convenient scale of equal parts of an inch to a foot, the length of every gore may be found with precision.

SAILS, GORED WITH A SWEEP on the head or the foot, or on both, have the depth of their gores marked on the selvage, from the square of the given depth on each cloth, and are cut as above; the longest selvage of one serving to measure the shortest selvage of the next, beginning with the first gored cloth next the middle in some sails, and the first cloth next the mast leech in others.

For those GORES that are IRREGULAR no strict rule can be given; they can only be determined by the judgment of the sail-maker, or by a drawing, and a scale of equal parts.

Although in the following directions the total amount of all sweep-gores is calculated at the rate of so many inches per cloth, each cloth has only such a gore as will form the sweep required.

The length of REEF and MIDDLE BANDS is governed by the width of the sail at their respective places; the LEECH-LININGS, BUNTLINE-CLOTHS, TOP-LININGS, MAST-CLOTHS, and CORNER-PIECES, are cut agreeably to the depth of the sail, and are particularly directed hereafter; each cloth and every article should be properly marked with charcoal, to prevent confusion or mistake.

Sails that have BONNETS are cut out the whole depth of the sail and bonnet included, allowing enough for the tablings on the foot of the sail, and head and foot of the bonnet. The bonnet is cut off after the sail is sewed together. If a DRABLER is required, it is allowed for in the cutting out the same as the bonnet.

SEAMS.

Sails have a double flat seam, and should be sewed with the best English-made twine of three threads, spun 360 fathoms to the pound, and have from one hundred and eight to one hundred and sixteen stitches in every yard in length.

The twine for large sails in the royal navy is waxed by hand, with genuine bees-wax, mixed with one-sixth part of clear turpentine; and, for small sails, in a mixture made with bees-wax, 4℔.; hogs-lard, 5℔.; and clear turpentine, 1℔. In the merchant-service the twine is dipped in tar, softened with a proper proportion of oil.

It is the erroneous practice of some sail-makers not to sew the seams any farther than where the edge is creased down for the tabling; but all sails should be sewed quite home to the end, and, when finished, should be well rubbed down with a rubber.

In the merchant-service the seams of particular sails, as boom or stay-sails, are made broader on the head, foot, or stay, according to the roach with which the sail is cut; this, in main-sails, try-sails, and all round-footed sails, is also used in the royal navy; and thus form what is called the belly, or bag part, of the sail. Boom main-sails, and the sails of sloops, generally have the seams broader at the foot than at the head, and broader at the head than in the middle.

The seams of courses and top-sails are stuck or stitched up, in the middle of the seams, along the whole length, with double seaming-twine; and have from 68 to 72 stitches in a yard. In the merchant-service, it is common to stick the seams with two rows of stitches, when the sail is half-worn, as they will then last till the sail is worn out.

The breadth of the seams of courses, top-sails, and other sails, in the royal navy, to be as follows, viz. courses and top-sails, for 50-gun ships and upwards, one inch and a half; and for 44-gun ships and under, one inch and a quarter, at head and foot: all other sails, one inch at head and foot.

TABLINGS.

The tablings of all sails are of a proportionable breadth to the size of the sail, and sewed at the edge with 68 to 72 stitches in a yard.

The Width of the TABLING *of all Sails in Inches.*

Names of the Sails.	Width on the Head of Square Sails, or Stay of Jibs and Stay-sails.	Width on the Foot.	Width on the Leeches of Square Sails, and Fore Leeches of Fore-and-aft Sails	Width on the After Leech.
Main & Fore Courses	From 4 to 6 Inc.	3 to 5	3 to 5	——
Sprit Courses	3 to 4	3 ——	3 ——	——
Mizen Courses	3 to 4	2 to 3	$3\frac{1}{2}$ to 4	3 Inches
Drivers and Spankers	3 to 4	2 to 3	$3\frac{1}{2}$ to 4	3 ——
Boom-sails	3 to 4	2 to 3	$3\frac{1}{2}$ to 4	3 ——
Top-sails	3 to $4\frac{1}{2}$	3 ——	3 ——	——
Sprit Top-sails	3 ——	$2\frac{1}{2}$ ——	$2\frac{1}{2}$ ——	——
Topgallant-sails	3 ——	$2\frac{1}{2}$ ——	$2\frac{1}{2}$ ——	——
Royals	$2\frac{1}{2}$ ——	2 ——	2 ——	——
Jibs	3 to $4\frac{1}{2}$	2 to $2\frac{1}{2}$	——	2 to 3
Stay-sails	3 to $4\frac{1}{2}$	2 to $2\frac{1}{2}$	——	2 to 3
Studding-sails	3 to 4	1 to 2	$1\frac{1}{2}$ to $2\frac{1}{2}$	——

LININGS.

Many sails have linings in various parts, to give them additional strength; such are the reef-bands, middle-bands, leech-linings, buntline-cloths, &c. all of which are particularly mentioned in their respective places. It may be necessary, however, to add here a few observations.

All linings are seamed on, and stuck with from 68 to 72 stitches per yard.

Top-linings and mast-cloths are put on the aft-side, and all other linings on the fore-sides, of sails.

Reef-bands should not be put on till the sail is sewed up; and it is the opinion of many, that middle-bands should not be put on till the sail is half worn.

HOLES.

Holes are made by an instrument called a pegging-awl, or a stabber, in large sails by a knife, and are fenced round by stitching the edge to a small grommet, made with log or other line; when finished, they should be well stretched or rounded up by a marling-spike or fid.

Sails have two holes in each cloth, at the heads and reefs of courses, top-sails, and other square sails; in the royal navy the heads of first and second reefs of top-sails have alternately two holes in one cloth and one in another; one hole in every yard in the stay of flying jibs; and one in every three-quarters of a yard in the stays of square tack and other stay-sails.

REEF and HEAD HOLES of large sails have grommets of 12-thread line, worked round with 18 to 21 stitches: small sails have grommets of 9-thread line, with 16 to 18 stitches, or as many as shall cover the line, and smaller holes in proportion.

In order to strengthen sails, it has been recommended to have the holes in the heads and reefs placed thus: one hole to be made in the seam, another in the middle of the canvas, and so on alternately; the hole in the seam to be half an inch lower than the hole in the middle of the canvas. By this the strain would lie upon the holes in the seam, which are more capable of bearing it than the holes in the middle of the single canvas.

It is likewise recommended to cut these holes with a hollow punch, instead of making them with a stabber or pricker. Cutting them with a knife, as used in the royal navy, answers the purpose.

The holes, for marling the clues of sails and the top-brims of top-sails, have grommets of log-line, and should have from 9 to 11 stitches: twelve holes are worked in each cloth.

Marling-holes of courses are at three-fourths of the depth of the tablings at the clues from the rope: and those of top-sails are at half the depth of the tablings at the clues, and top-brim, from the rope.

BOLT-ROPE.

Bolt-rope should be well made of fine yarn, spun from the best Riga rhine hemp, well topped, and sewed on with good English-made twine of three threads, spun 200 fathoms to the pound: the twine in the royal navy is dipped in a composition made of beeswax, 4lb.; hog's-lard, 5lb.; and clear turpentine, 1lb.; and, in the merchant-service, in tar softened with oil.

Bolt-ropes should be stoved in a stove by the heat of a flue, and not in a baker's oven or a stove tub; and tarred in the best Stockholm tar. The flexibility of them should be always considered, in taking in the slack, which must rest on the judgment of the sail-maker.

The clues and top-brims should be wormed and served, or wormed, parcelled, and served, while the bolt-rope is sewing to the sail, and before both parts are confined.

The Number of Yarns in each Strand of Bolt-Ropes, and Threads for sewing them on, required for Sails in the Royal Navy.

Size of the Rope in Inches.	Threads in each Strand.	Threads to sew them on. Ordinary	Extra.	Size of the Rope in Inches.	Threads in each Strand.	Threads to sew them on. Ordinary	Extra.
6	98	10	2	3¼	29	4	2
5¾	90	10	0	3	25	4	2
5½	83	10	0	2¾	21	4	0
5¼	75	8	2	2½	17	4	0
5	68	8	2	2¼	14	2	2
4¾	62	8	0	2	11	2	2
4½	56	8	0	1¾	9	2	0
4¼	50	6	2	1½	7	2	0
4	44	6	2	1¼	5	2	0
3¾	39	6	0	1	3	2	0
3½	34	6	0	—	—	—	—

Bolt-ropes of all sails should be neatly sewed on through every contline of the rope; and, to avoid stretching, the rope must be kept tightly twisted while sewing on, and care taken that neither too much nor too little slack is taken in: they are to be cross-stitched at the leeches, every 12 inches in length; at every seam, and in the middle of every cloth at the foot, with three cross-stitches: four cross-stitches should be taken at all beginnings and fastenings off; the first stitch given twice, and the last three times. Small sails have two cross-stitches at every seam, and three at every fastening-off.

Annexed is a Table of the sizes of bolt-ropes of every sail.

A TABLE of the Circumference in Inches of BOLT-ROPE for Sails of Ships of each Class, Sloops, Brigs, Cutters & Boats.

NAMES OF THE SAILS.	Sloops. Rope.				Brigs. Rope.				Tons. 1200. Rope.				Tons. 700. Rope.				Tons. 500. Rope.				Tons. 300. Rope.			
	Head or Stay	Foot	Fore-Leech	After-Leech	Head or Stay	Foot	Fore-Leech	After-Leech	Head or Stay	Foot	Fore-Leech	After-Leech	Head or Stay	Foot	Fore-Leech	After-Leech	Head or Stay	Foot	Fore-Leech	After-Leech	Head or Stay	Foot	Fore-Leech	After-Leech
	In																							
Main-Course or Main-Sail	1½	3½	3½	3½	1½	3	3½	2	2¼	5½	5½	5½	1¾	4½	4½	4½	1½	4	4	4	1½	3½	3½	3½
Fore-Course	1½	3	3	3	1½	3	3	3	2	5	5	5	1¾	4	4	4	1½	3½	3½	3½	1½	3	3	3
Mizen-Course	1½	1¾	2¼	1¾	—	—	—	—	1¾	3	3½	3	1½	2¼	2¾	2¼	1½	2	2½	2	1½	1¾	2¼	1¾
Main-Top-Sail	1½	3	2½	2½	1¼	3	2½	2½	2	5	4¼	4¼	1¾	4¼	3½	3½	1¾	3¾	3	3	1½	3¼	2½	2½
Fore-Top-Sail	1¼	2¾	2¼	2¼	1¼	2¾	2¼	2¼	1¾	4½	3¾	3¾	1½	3¾	3	3	1½	3¼	2¾	2¾	1¼	2¾	2½	2½
Mizen-Top-Sail	1¼	2¼	1¾	1¾	—	—	—	—	1½	3¼	2½	2½	1½	3	2½	2½	1¼	2¾	2¼	2¼	1¼	2¼	1¾	1¾
Sprit-Sail-Course	1¼	1¾	1¾	1¾	—	—	—	—	1½	3	3	3	1½	2¼	2¼	2¼	1½	2	2	2	1¼	1¾	1¾	1¾
Sprit-Top-Sail, Main and Fore-Top-Gallant-Sail	1	1½	1½	1½	1	1½	1½	1½	1½	2½	2½	2½	1¼	2	2	2	1¼	1¾	1¾	1¾	1	1½	1½	1½
Main and Fore-Stay-Sail	2	2	—	2	2	2	—	2	3	3	—	3	2½	2½	—	2½	2¼	2¼	—	2¼	2	2	—	2
Fore-Top-Mast-Stay-Sail	2	2	—	2	1¾	1¾	—	1¾	2½	2½	—	2½	2¼	2¼	—	2¼	2	2	—	2	2	2	—	2
Main-Top-Mast-Stay-Sail	2	1¼	1¼	1¼	2	1¼	1¼	1¼	3	1¾	1¾	1¾	2½	1½	1½	1½	2¼	1½	1½	1½	2	1¼	1¼	1¼
Middle-Stay-Sail	1¾	1¼	1¼	1¼	1¾	1¼	1¼	1¼	2¾	1¾	1¾	1¾	2¼	1½	1½	1½	2	1½	1½	1½	1¾	1¼	1¼	1¼
Mizen-Stay-Sail	2	2	2	2	—	—	—	—	3	3	3	3	2½	2½	2½	2½	2¼	2¼	2¼	2¼	2	2	2	2
Main-Top-Gallant and Mizen-Top-Stay-Sail	1¾	1¼	1¼	1¼	—	—	—	—	2½	1½	1½	1½	2	1¼	1¼	1¼	1¾	1¼	1¼	1¼	1¾	1¼	1¼	1¼
Main, Fore, and Top-Mast-Studding-Sail	1	1½	1½	1½	1	1½	1½	1½	1¼	2	2	2	1¼	1¾	1¾	1¾	1¼	1¾	1¾	1¾	1	1½	1½	1½
Top-Gallant-Studding, Mizen-Top-Gallant-Sail, Main and Fore-Royal	1	1¼	1¼	1¼	1	1¼	1¼	1¼	1¼	1¾	1¾	1¾	1	1½	1½	1½	1	1¼	1¼	1¼	1	1¼	1¼	1¼
Mizen-Royal	¾	1	1	1	—	—	—	—	1	1½	1½	1½	1	1¼	1¼	1¼	¾	1	1	1	¾	1	1	1
Jib	2¼	1¼	—	1¼	2¼	1¼	—	1¼	3	1½	—	1½	2¾	1½	—	1½	2½	1¼	—	1½	2¼	1¼	—	1¼
Driver-Sail	1½	2	2	2	—	—	—	—	1½	2½	2½	2½	1¼	2¼	2¼	2¼	1¼	2¼	2¼	2¼	1½	2	2	2

CUTTERS.	Head or Stay	Foot	Fore-Leech	After-Leech
Main-Sail	1½	1¾	3	1¾
Try-Sail, or Storm Main-Sail	1½	1¾	3	1¾
Top-Sail	1½	2¼	2¼	2¼
Save-all Top-Sail	1	1½	1½	1½
Square Sail	1½	2¼	2¼	2¼
Gaff Top-Sail	1	1¾	2¼	1¾
Fore-Sail	3	2	—	2
Storm Fore-Sail	3½	2¾	—	1¾
Ringtail-Sail	½	1½	1½	1½
Water-Sail	1¾	2¼	2¼	2¼
First Jib	6	4	—	1½
2d and 3d Jibs	6	4	—	1½
Storm Jib	5	3½	—	1½
BOATS' SAILS.				
Lateen-Sail	1	1½	—	1½
Settee-Sail	1	1½	—	1½
Lug-Sail	1	1½	1½	1½
Sprit-Sail	1¼	1¼	1¼	1¼
Jib	1½	1	—	1
Fore-Sail	1¾	1	1	1

A TABLE of the Circumference in Inches of Bolt-Rope for Sails of Ships of each Class, Sloops, Brigs, Cutters & Boats.

(Table, rotated 90°. Reproduced as best as readable.)

NAMES OF THE SAILS.	Sloops. Rope. Head or Stay / Foot / Fore-Leech / After-Leech	Brigs. Rope. Head or Stay / Foot / Fore-Leech / After-Leech	Tons. 1200. Rope. Head or Stay / Foot / Fore-Leech / After-Leech	Tons. 700. Rope. Head or Stay / Foot / Fore-Leech / After-Leech	Tons. 500. Rope. Head or Stay / Foot / Fore-Leech / After-Leech	Tons. 300. Rope. Head or Stay / Foot / Fore-Leech / After-Leech	CUTTERS.	Head or Stay / Foot / Fore-Leech / After-Leech
Main-Course or Main-Sail	In 1¾ 3½ 3½ 1½	1¼ 3 3 2	2¼ 5½ 5½ 5½	1½ 4½ 4½ 4¾	1¼ 4 4 4	1¼ 3½ 3½ 3½	Main-Sail	1½ 1¾ 1¾ 1¾
Fore-Course	1½ 3 3 1½	1¼ 3 3 3	2 5 5 5	1½ 4 4 4	1¼ 3½ 3½ 3½	1½ 3 3 3	Try-Sail, or Storm Main-Sail	1¼ 1¾ 1¾ 1¾
Mizen-Course	1¼ 1¾ 2 1¾	1¼ 3 3 2¼	1½ 3 3 3½	1½ 2¾ 2¾ 2¾	1½ 3 3 2	1¼ 1¾ 1¾ 2¼	Top-Sail	1½ 2½ 2½ 2¼
Main-Top-Sail	1½ 3 2¼ 2¼	1¼ 3 2¾ 2¼	2 5 4¾ 3¾	1¾ 4¾ 3¾ 3½	1½ 3½ 3 3	1¾ 3½ 2½ 2¼	Save-all Top-Sail	1 1½ 1½ 1½
Fore-Top-Sail	1¼ 2¾ 2¼ 2¼	1¼ 2½ 2¼ 2¼	1¾ 4¼ 3¾ 3¾	1½ 3¾ 3 3	1¾ 3¼ 2½ 2½	1¾ 3¼ 2¾ 2¾	Square Sail	1½ 2¼ 2¼ 2¼
Mizen-Top-Sail	1¼ 2¼ 1¾ 1¾		1¾ 3¼ 2½ 2½	1½ 3 2¼ 2¼	1¼ 2¾ 2¼ 2¼	1¼ 2¼ 1½ 1½	Gaff Top-Sail	1 1¾ 2¾ 1¾
Sprit-Sail-Course	1¼ 1¾ 1¾ 1¾		1¼ 3 2 2	1¼ 3 2 2	1½ 3 2 2	1½ 2½ 1½ 1½	Fore-Sail	3 2 — 2
Sprit-Top-Sail, Main and Fore-Top-Gallant-Sail	1 1½ 1¼ 1¼	1 1¾ 1¾ 1¼	1¼ 2¼ 2 2¼	2 2¼ 2 1¾	1¼ 1¾ 1½ 1¾	1¼ 1¾ 1¼ 1¼	Storm Fore-Sail	3½ 2¼ — 1¾
Main and Fore-Stay-Sail	2 2 2 2	1¾ 2 2 2	1¾ 3 2 2	2½ 2¼ 2 2	2½ 2½ 2 2½	2 2 — 2	Ringtail-Sail	¾ 1¼ 1½ 1½
Fore-Top-Mast-Stay-Sail	2 2 2 2	1¾ 1½ 1¾ 1¾	1½ 2½ 2½ 2¼	2¼ 2¼ 2 2¼	2 2 2 2	2 1¾ 1¾ 2	Water-Sail	1¾ 2½ 2¾ 2¼
Main-Top-Mast-Stay-Sail	2 2 1¾ 1¾	1¼ 1¼ 1½ 1½	2 2¾ 2½ 2¼	2¼ 2¼ 2 2¼	2 1¾ 1¾ 2	2 1¾ 1¾ 2	First Jib	6 4 — 1¾
Middle-Stay-Sail	1½ 1¾ 1¼ 1¼	1¼ 1½ 1¾ 1¾	1½ 1¾ 1¾ 1¾	1¾ 1½ 1½ 1¾	1½ 1½ 1½ 1½	1¾ 1¾ 1¾ 1¾	2d and 3d Jibs	6 4 — 1¾
Mizen-Stay-Sail	2 2 1¾ 1¾		1¾ 3 3 3	2¼ 2¼ 2¼ 2¼	2¼ 2¼ 2¼ 2¼	2 2 2 2	Storm Jib	5 3½ — 1½
Main-Top-Gallant and Mizen-Top-Stay-Sail	1¾ 1¼ 1¼ 1¾	1 1¾ 1¾ 1¾	2¼ 2¼ 2¼ 2 1¾	1¾ 1½ 1½ 1¾	1½ 1¾ 1½ 1¾	1¾ 1¾ 1¾ 1¾	BOATS' SAILS.	
Main, Fore, and Top-Mast-Studding-Sail	1 1¼ 1½ 1¾		1¾ 2 2 1¾	2 1¾ 1¾ 1¾	1½ 1½ 1¾ 1¾	1 1½ 1¼ 1¼	Lateen-Sail	1 1½ 1½ 1½
Top-Gallant-Studding, Mizen-Top-Gallant-Sail, Main and Fore-Royal	1 1¼ 1¼ 1¼	1 1¼ 1¼ 1¼	1 1¾ 1½ 1½	1 1¼ 1½ 1½	1 1 1¼ 1¼	1 1¼ 1¼ 1¼	Settee-Sail	1 1½ 1¾ 1¾
Mizen-Royal	¾ 1 1 1		1 1¾ 1¾ 1½	1 1¼ 1¼ 1¼	¾ 1 1 1	¾ 1 1 1	Lug-Sail	1 1¾ 1¼ 1¼
Jib	2¼ 1¼ 1¾ 2½	2¼ 1¾ 1¾ 1¾	2½ 2½ 2¼ 2¼	1½ 2 1½ 1¾	1¾ 2¼ 1¾ 1¾	1¾ 2¼ 1¾ 1¾	Sprit-Sail	1¾ 1¼ 1¼ 1¼
Driver-Sail	1¾ 2 2 2	1¼ 1¼ 1¼ 1¾	1½ 2¼ 2¼ 2¼	1¼ 2¼ 2¼ 2¼	1½ 2¼ 2¼ 2¼	1½ 2 2 2	Jib	1½ 1 — 1
							Fore-Sail	1¼ 1 1 1

CLUES.

The CLUES of large sails are made of rope, called a clue-rope, which splices into the bolt-rope, with a tapering splice; but the clues of smaller sails are formed with the bolt-rope only.

The CLUES of MAIN-COURSES are made with clue-rope, 2 inches larger than the bolt-rope, for ships of 50 guns and upwards, and 1½ inch larger for ships under 50 guns; and those for the merchant-service are in proportion. The clue-rope splices into the foot-rope at the first buntline cringle, and into the leech-rope at the lower bowline cringle: it is wormed with three-quarter ratline, or sizeable spunyarn; then parcelled over with worn canvas, well tarred, and served over that with spunyarn: it is then marled on to the sail with marline, or houseline, as far as it is served. Fourteen turns or twists of the strands in the length of the clue-rope being left to form the clue, it is seized with several turns of inch, or other suitable line, and strained tight with three or more cross turns.

The CLUES of FORE-COURSES are made with clue-rope, being larger than the bolt-rope in the same proportion as the clue-ropes of main-courses. It splices into the foot-rope at the first buntline cringle, and into the leech-rope at one-eighth of the depth from the foot. It is prepared and fastened in other respects like the clue-rope of main-courses.

The CLUES of MIZEN-COURSES are made with clue-rope, half an inch larger than the foot-rope, and three fathoms in length. It splices into the foot-rope at three feet from the clue; then, leaving sufficient length for a nine-inch clue, it splices into the after-leech rope at a proper distance. It is wormed, parcelled, and served, as that of the main-course, at the clue, and two feet each way from the clue: it is then marled on to the sail, the length of the serving; and the clue is seized with three-quarter ratline.

The CLUES of MAIN and FORE-TOP-SAILS are made of the foot-rope, which is left sufficiently long to form the clues, and splice into the leech-rope at the lower bowline cringle. It is wormed, parcelled, and served, at the clues, and three feet each way from them: it is marled on to the sail for the extent of the serving on each side the clues, which are seized as those of main and fore courses.

The CLUES of MIZEN-TOP-SAILS are similar to those of main and fore top-sails, except that the foot-rope is wormed, parcelled, and served, at the clues, and two feet each way from them.

The CLUES of TOP-GALLANT SAILS and ROYALS are made of the bolt-rope, which is sewed home to the clues: the clues only are wormed and served with spunyarn, and seized with small line.

The CLUES of MAIN, FORE, and MIZEN STAY-SAILS; MAIN and FORE TOP-MAST-STAY-SAILS; MIDDLE STAY-SAILS; SPANKERS; and DRIVERS. These are made with clue-rope, half an inch larger than the foot-rope, and two fathoms long: it is wormed, parcelled, and served, at the clue and two feet each way from the clue: it splices into the foot and after leech-rope, equally distant from the clue: it is marled on to the sail for the extent of the serving, and the clue is seized as the clues of courses are.

The CLUES of MIZEN-TOP-MAST-STAY-SAILS; TOP-GALLANT-STAY-SAILS; all STUDDING-SAILS; SPRIT-SAIL-TOP-SAILS; SLOOPS' SAVE-ALL-TOP-SAILS, TOP-GALLANT-SAILS, WATER-SAILS, and RING-TAIL-SAILS; are made of the bolt-rope, which is sewed home to the clues; the clues only are wormed, and served with spunyarn, and seized with suitable line.

The CLUES of SPRIT-SAIL-COURSES are made of the bolt-rope; wormed, parcelled, and served, in large ships, (but served only in small ships); at the clue and two feet each way from the clue; it is marled on to the sail to the extent of the serving, and the clue is seized as those of other courses are.

The CLUES of BRIGS' MAIN-SAILS; CUTTERS' MAIN-SAILS and TRY-SAILS; SLOOPS' MAIN-SAILS and TRY-SAILS; SLOOPS' FORE-SAILS, JIBS, and STORM-JIBS; SMACKS, MAIN-SAILS, FORE-SAILS, and JIBS; are formed by having a thimble stuck through cringle-holes.

The CLUES of SLOOPS' SQUARE-SAILS, TOP-SAILS, GAFF TOP-SAILS, are sometimes made with clue-rope two inches and a half in circumference, which is marled on to the sail, and served for the extent of the marling-holes. When they are not made with clue-rope, as in small sails, the bolt-rope is sewed home to the clues, and the clues served.

The CLUES of SLOOPS' FLYING-JIBS are sometimes made of the

foot-rope, which splices into the leech-rope at one yard up from the clue, and is served and seized at the clue. Thimbles are sometimes stuck in to form the clues.

The CLUES of BOATS' and other small sails are made of the bolt-rope, sewed home to the clues, and seized with small lines.

CRINGLES.

EARING-CRINGLES are made of an additional length (of 14 twists or turns) of the leech-rope left at the head of the sail, which being turned back, forms the cringle by splicing its end into the leech-rope, and cross-stitching the whole of the splice; the first stitch to be given twice, and the last stitch three times.

CRINGLES should be made of the strands of new bolt-rope, half-an-inch smaller than the bolt-rope on the sail, in which they are stuck.

Splices are made by opening the ends of two ropes, and placing the strands between each other; openings being made in the un-

twisted part of the rope nearest the end with a marling-spike, the strands are thrust through them; and the large ends are regularly tapered from the middle by cutting away some of the yarns every time they are thrust through. The small strands, as those of the foot or leech-rope, are stuck twice through the openings made in the large rope; and the large strands are stuck three times through the leech or foot-rope. The middle strand of the taper, being the longest, is stuck in last, and once more than the others. All splices are cross-stitched as far as they run.

REEF and REEF-TACKLE PENDANT CRINGLES are stuck through holes made in the tablings, and the lower ends are put through the bolt-rope once more than the upper ends, being more liable to be drawn out.

The openings of BOWLINE and BUNTLINE CRINGLES are at the distance of four turns or twists of the strands in the bolt-rope asunder, and the ends are first stuck in an opening made with a marling-spike, under two strands of the bolt-rope; then passing over the next, they are stuck under one strand, and again passing over another, they are finally stuck under the next. The ends of the buntline cringles, next the service of the clues of courses, should be left long enough to be worked under the service, to meet or reach the ends of the clue-rope.

BONNET AND DRABLER.

Bonnets have a head-tabling, to which a line that forms the latchings is sewed in bights. These latchings are six inches asunder, and six inches long, except the two middle ones, which are twelve inches long, to fasten off with. In fastening it, the loops are alternately reeved through holes in the foot of the sail, and through each other, and fasten by the two long loops in the middle with two half-hitches, by loosing of which they unreeve themselves. The leeches and foot are tabled, &c. similar to the foot of the sail the bonnet is intended for. The DRABLER is similar to a bonnet, under which it is placed by means of latchings, as the bonnet is to the foot of the sail.

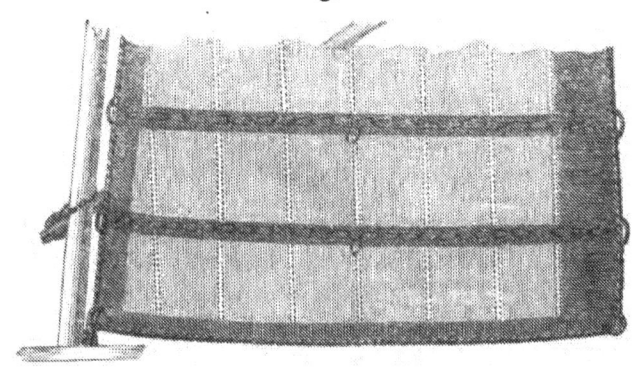

REEF-HANKS.

In lieu of points there are used, on some sails, mentioned particularly hereafter, REEF-HANKS, which are pieces of log-line (reef-points for ships' sails are made of much larger line than log) sewed on to the reef-band, at each seam, on both sides. One end of each hank is spread open, and sewed on securely, as represented in the adjoining figure: the other end of each hank is whipped. Or they may be thus fixed on: the line is thrust through the sail, and securely sewed to it on one side, by opening the strands a little, so as to lay them flat upon the canvas.

IMPROVEMENTS SUGGESTED IN THE PRACTICE OF SAIL-MAKING.

Much advantage would frequently result to the naval service, if many of the sails of ships were made of equal size; so that, in cases of necessity, they might be interchangeably used. Thus, the mizen-top-sail being, at present, nearly the size of the main-top-gallant-sail, there seems no reason why the yards, masts, and of course the sails, should not be made to suit each other.

The main and fore top-sails only differ, in general, one cloth, or about two feet, at head and foot, and in depth from one to three feet; the masts, yards, and sails, might here be made alike; as, indeed, is generally the practice in brigs, and was first introduced in the North-country trade.

The main and fore top-gallant-sails differ very little in depth, and only one cloth, or about two feet, at head and foot: these might easily be made alike.

The mizen-top-gallant-sail and main and fore royal might be brought to the same dimensions.

The main-sail and fore-sail might be made alike as to their head; but, as the main-sail has a gore at the leech, and a larger gore at the foot, in order to clear it of the gallows, boats, &c. which the fore-sail has not, it may be more difficult to arrange them: but if much convenience is found in the sails named above, this might be obviated in time.

The number of sails in a vessel takes up considerable room; they are put all together, in a sail-room or cabin, and create confusion in getting out; and in the event of losing sails by stress of weather, and in long voyages, the above alterations might be very useful.

Top-mast-studding-sails, as well as lower studding-sails, are occasionally substituted for awnings; they might, by a very little attention in planning the rigging of a ship, be made so as to answer both uses.

Probably these hints would be attended with more advantage in the merchant-service than in the royal navy, because a merchant-ship is not often so plentifully stored with spare sails as ships of the British navy.

RULES

FOR ASCERTAINING

THE QUANTITY OF CANVAS CONTAINED IN THE DIFFERENT SAILS.

CANVAS 24 inches wide is used for the royal navy, and is certainly the strongest. Various widths of canvas are used in the merchant-service, from 24 to 36 inches. The following rules are adapted equally to all widths, although the examples are calculated for canvas of 24 inches.

RULE I.

To find the Quantity of Canvas in Main and Fore Courses; Main, Fore, Mizen, and Sprit-Sails; Top-Sails; Top-Gallant-Sails; Royals; Top-Mast-Studding-Sails; Top-Gallant-Studding-Sails; Sloops' Top-Sails; Sloops' Save-all-Top-Sails; and Sloops' Top-Gallant-Sails.

Add the number of cloths in the head and foot, and halve the product to make it square; then multiply by the depth of the middle cloth; and add the quantity in the linings, bands, and pieces, and the quantity in the foot-gores, when the foot is cut hollow.

To find the quantity in the foot-gores, add together the number of inches gored on each cloth on one side of the sail, and multiply the product by half the number of gored cloths, and divide by 36, to bring that into yards.

Example of a Main-Course for a Ship of 20 Guns.

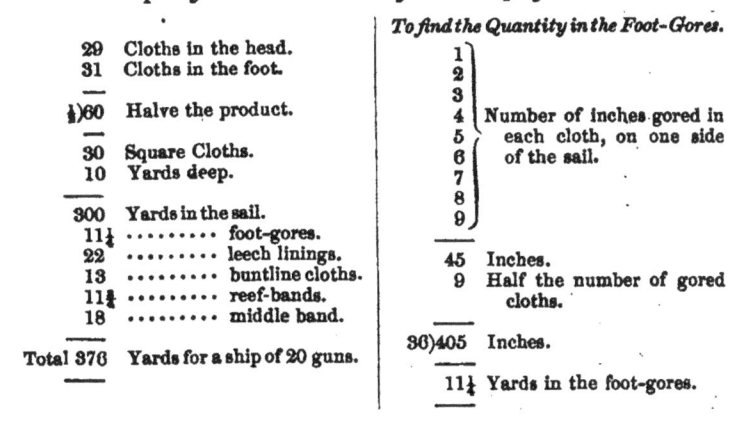

29	Cloths in the head.	*To find the Quantity in the Foot-Gores.*	
31	Cloths in the foot.	1	
½)60	Halve the product.	2	
		3	
30	Square Cloths.	4	Number of inches gored in each cloth, on one side of the sail.
10	Yards deep.	5	
		6	
300	Yards in the sail.	7	
11¼	········ foot-gores.	8	
22	········ leech linings.	9	
13	········ buntline cloths.	45	Inches.
11¾	········ reef-bands.	9	Half the number of gored cloths.
18	········ middle band.		
Total 376	Yards for a ship of 20 guns.	36)405	Inches.
		11¼	Yards in the foot-gores.

Example of a Main-Top-Mast-Studding-Sail, for a 20 Gun Ship, having no Foot-Gores.

```
        8   Cloths in the head.
       12   Cloths in the foot.
      ────
     ½)20   Halve the product.
      ────
       10   Square cloths.
       14   Yards deep.
      ────
      140
        1¼  Yard in the reef-band.
      ────
  Total 141¼
```

RULE II.

To find the Quantity of Canvas in Mizen Courses.

Add the depth of the fore and after leech together, and halve the product for a medium depth; then multiply the medium depth by the number of cloths; and add to that the additional canvas contained in the foot-gores, linings, bands, and pieces.

To find the quantity in the foot-gores.—The number of cloths in the sail must be multiplied by the additional length that the square cloth in the middle is more than those at the tack and clue; then, the gores to the tack and clue being subtracted, the remainder is the answer in inches, and which, divided by 36, gives the quantity in yards.

Example of a Mizen Course for a Ship of 20 Guns.

13¼	Yards, depth of the after-leech.	*To find the Quantity in the Foot-Gores.*	
8	Yards, depth of the mast-leech.	10	Number of cloths.
½)21¼	Halve the product.	10	Inches, depth of the square cloth below the depth at the tack.
10⅝	Medium depth.		
10	Number of cloths.	100	
107½	Yards in the sail.	20	Inches, gores to the tack and clue.
2	.... reef-band.		
7	.... pieces.	36)80	Inches.
2¼	.... foot-gores.		
Total 118¾	Yards for a ship of 20 guns.	2¼	Yards nearly in the foot-gores.

RULE III.

To find the Quantity of Canvas contained in Jibs; Main and Fore Stay-Sails; Fore-Top-Mast-Stay-Sails; Storm-Mizens; Sky-Scrapers; Boats' Fore-Sails; and Boats' Lateen Sails.

Multiply half the number of cloths by the depth of the leech, and add the quantity in the pieces, and in the foot-gores, when cut with a gore on the foot.

To find the quantity in the foot-gores.—Multiply half the number of cloths in the foot by the regular gore per cloth, and that product multiplied by the whole number of cloths in the foot, gives the answer in inches, which divide by 36 to bring into yards.

Example of a Main-Stay-Sail for a Ship of 20 Guns.

11	Half the number of cloths.
10	Yards, depth of the leech.
110	Yards in the sail.
4	.... pieces.
Total 114	Yards for a 20-gun-ship.

Example of a Jib for a 20-Gun Ship.

18 Yards, depth of the leech.	*To find the quantity in the foot-gores.*
9½ Half the number of cloths.	
———	9½ Half the number of cloths.
171 Yards.	3 Inches gore per cloth.
4 ..... in the pieces.	———
15 .... foot-gores.	28½
———	19 Cloths in the foot.
Total 190 Yards.	———
	36)541½ Inches.
	———
	15 Yards.

RULE IV.

To find the quantity of Canvas contained in Mizen-Stay-Sails; Main-Top-Mast-Stay-Sails; Mizen-Top-Mast-Stay-Sails; Sloops' Gaff-Top-Sails; Sloops' Ring-Tail-Sails; Boats' Settee-Sails; Boats' Main, Fore, and Mizen, Sprit-Sails.

Add the depth of the tack, bunt, or fore-leech, to the depth of the after-leech, and halve them for a medium depth: add the number of cloths in the head and foot together, and halve them, to reduce them square; then multiply the number of squared cloths by the medium depth; and add to that the additional canvas contained in the linings, bands, and pieces.

Example of a Mizen-Top-Mast-Stay-Sail for a Ship of 20 Guns.

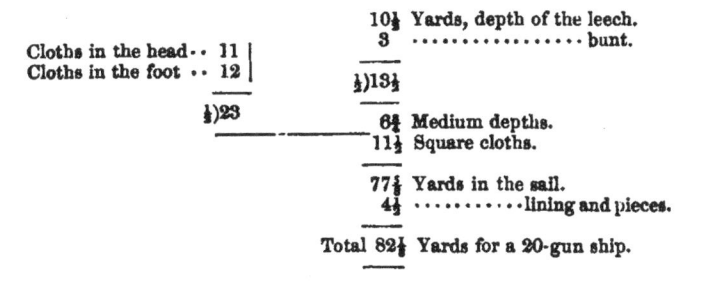

	10½ Yards, depth of the leech.
Cloths in the head ·· 11	3 .... bunt.
Cloths in the foot ·· 12	———
	½)13½
½)23	———
	6¾ Medium depths.
	11½ Square cloths.
	———
	77⅝ Yards in the sail.
	4½ .... lining and pieces.
	———
	Total 82⅛ Yards for a 20-gun ship.

F

RULE V.

To find the Quantity of Canvas contained in Middle-Stay-Sails and Main-Top-Gallant-Stay-Sails.

Add the depth of the bunt to the depth of the leech, and halve the same for a medium depth; then multiply the medium depth by the number of cloths, and add the quantity in the lining and pieces.

Example of a Middle-Stay-Sail for a Ship of 20 Guns.

```
    10¼  Yards, depth of the leech.
     4¼  ................ bunt.
   ½)14½ Halve the product.
     7¼  Medium depth.
    16   Number of cloths.

   116   Yards in the sail.
     5¼  .......... lining and pieces.
Total 121¼ Yards for a 20-gun ship.
```

RULE VI.

To find the Quantity of Canvas contained in Lower Studding-Sails; Sprit-Sail-Courses; Sloops' Square-Sails, or Cross-Jack; and Sloops' Water-Sails.

Multiply the number of cloths by the shortest depth, and add the quantity in the bands and pieces, and the quantity in the foot-gores, when the foot is cut hollow.

To find the quantity of the foot-gores. Add together the gores on each cloth on one side of the sail, and multiply that sum by half the number of gored cloths.

Example of a Lower Main-Studding-Sail for a Ship of 20 Guns.

```
    13   Yards deep.
    12   Number of cloths.

   156   Yards in the sails.
     1¾  .......... reef-band.
     1   .......... pieces.
Total 158¾ Yards.
```

IN THE DIFFERENT SAILS.

Example of a Sloop's Square-Sail, having a hollow Foot.

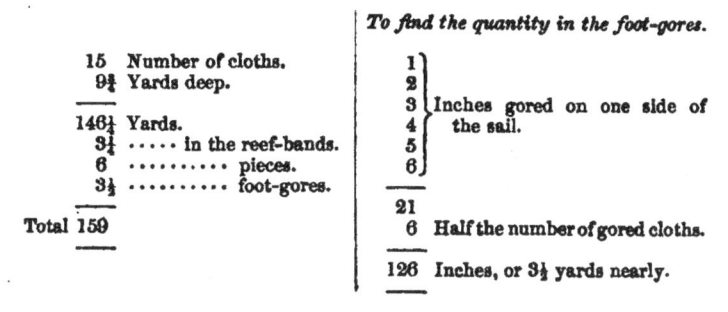

15	Number of cloths.		*To find the quantity in the foot-gores.*
9¾	Yards deep.	1	
146¼	Yards.	2	
3¼	..... in the reef-bands.	3	Inches gored on one side of the sail.
6	.... pieces.	4	
3½	.... foot-gores.	5	
		6	
Total 159		21	
		6	Half the number of gored cloths.
		126	Inches, or 3½ yards nearly.

RULE VII.

To find the Quantity of Canvas contained in Spankers, Driver Boom-Sails; Brigs' Main-Sails; Cutters' Main-Sails; Cutters' Try-Sails; Sloops' Main-Sails; Sloops' Try-Sails; and Smacks' Main-Sails.

Add together the number of cloths in the head and foot, and halve the product to make it square; add together the depth of the fore and after-leeches, and halve that sum for a medium depth; then multiply the number of square cloths by the medium depth; and add the quantity in the pieces and foot-gores.

To find the quantity in the foot-gores. Add together the gores from the tack to the first square cloth in the foot, and multiply half the sum by the number of cloths in the foot: then (if there are gores to the clue) add together the gores from the clue to the first square cloth in the foot, and multiply half the sum by the number of cloths gored to the clue; which, subtracted from the product of the gores to the tack, gives the answer.

THE QUANTITY OF CANVAS

Example of a Cutter's Main-Sail.

To find the quantity in the foot-gores.

```
                              Inches.                    24 Yards, depth of the
  Inches.                ¼)110 Gores to the tack.            after-leech.
¼)20 Gores to the clue.       ──                         18 ·········fore-leech.
     ──                       55                            ──
     10                       30 Cloths in the foot.     ¼)42
     13 Cloths gored to the   ──
        clue.                 1650 Inches.               21 Yards, medium depth.
    130 Inches subtracted.     130                       26 Square cloths.
                              ──
                           36)1520 Inches.               546
                              ──                         53¼ Yards in the reef-
                              42¼ Yards.─────────            bands, linings, and
                                                             pieces.
                                                         42¼ Yards in the foot-
                                                             gores.
                                                    Total 642 Yards.
```

RULE VIII.

To find the Quantity of Canvas in Sloops' Fore-Sails; Sloops' Jibs; Sloops' Storm-Jibs; Sloops' Flying-Jibs; Smacks' Fore-Sails; Smacks' Jibs; Boats' Jibs.

Multiply half the number of cloths in the sail by the depth of the leech, and add the quantity in the foot-gores, bands, and pieces.

To find the quantity in the foot-gores. Multiply the number of cloths by the depth of the gores when added together; and five-eighths of the product is the answer.

Example of a Sloop's Fore-Sail.

```
                                    To find the quantity in the foot-gores.
    4  Half the number of cloths.
   11½ Yards, depth of the leech.      Gores.       ⎱ Total, 21 Inches.
   ──                                1, 2, 3, 4, 5, 6, ⎰
   46  Yards.                       ──
    3  ·····in the foot-gores.          21 Inches.
    6¼ ········bands and pieces.         8 Number of cloths.
                                        ──
Total 55¼ Yards.                     ⅝)168
                                        ──
                                       105 Inches, or 3 yards, nearly.
```

RULE IX.

To find the Quantity of Canvas in Boats' Lug-Sails.

Add together the number of cloths in the head and foot, and halve the sum to make it square: add the depth of the leeches together, and halve the sum for a medium depth: then multiply the number of square cloths by the medium depth, and add the quantity in the foot-gores and reef-bands.

To find the quantity in the foot-gores. Multiply the number of gored cloths to the tack by the foot-gore on the cloth next the tack.

EXAMPLE.

	6	Square cloths.
	4	Yards, medium depth.
	24	Yards.
	3¼	..... in the foot-gores.
	1	.... reef-bands.
Total	28¼	Yards.

To find the quantity in the foot-gores.

5 Number of cloths gored to the tack.
20 Inches; gore on the cloth next the tack.
Total 100 Inches, or little more than 2 yards and three-quarters.

The Number of Reefs, Points, Rope-Bands, and Gaskets, in fitting each of the under-mentioned Sails.

Number of Guns.	Sprit-sail Course. Reefs	Points	Rope-Bands	Gaskets	Fore-Course. Reefs	Points	Rope-Bands	Gaskets	Main-Course. Reefs	Points	Rope-Bands	Gaskets	Total of the Courses. Reefs	Points	Rope-Bands	Gaskets	Fore Top-Sail. Reefs	Points	Rope-Bands	Gaskets	Main Top-Sail. Reefs	Points	Rope-Bands	Gaskets	Mizen Top-Sail. Reefs	Points	Rope-Bands	Gaskets	Total of the Top-Sails. Reefs	Points	Rope-Bands	Gaskets
100	1	64	64	6	1	90	90	8	1	102	102	8	3	256	256	22	3	180	52	6	3	210	61	6	2	92	42	4	8	482	155	16
90	1	60	60	6	1	86	88	8	1	98	98	8	3	244	244	22	3	171	50	6	3	198	58	6	2	88	40	4	8	457	148	16
80	1	58	58	6	1	82	82	8	1	94	94	8	3	234	234	22	3	165	48	6	3	192	56	6	2	86	40	4	8	443	144	16
74	1	62	62	6	1	86	86	8	1	98	98	8	3	246	246	22	3	177	52	6	3	204	60	6	2	90	41	4	8	471	153	16
70	1	58	58	6	1	82	82	8	1	92	92	8	3	232	232	22	3	165	49	6	3	189	56	6	2	85	39	4	8	439	144	16
64	1	58	58	6	1	80	80	8	1	92	92	8	3	230	230	22	3	165	49	6	3	189	56	6	2	85	39	4	8	439	144	16
60	1	54	54	6	1	78	78	8	1	88	88	8	3	220	220	22	3	156	45	6	3	180	52	6	2	80	36	4	8	416	133	16
50	1	52	52	4	1	72	72	6	1	82	82	6	3	206	206	16	3	147	43	4	3	168	49	4	2	72	33	4	8	387	125	12
44	1	46	46	4	1	66	66	6	1	74	74	6	3	186	186	16	3	135	39	4	3	150	44	4	2	66	30	2	8	351	113	10
38 & 36	1	50	50	4	2	132	66	6	2	152	76	6	5	334	192	16	3	138	41	4	3	153	46	4	2	70	33	2	8	361	120	10
32	1	50	50	4	2	128	64	6	2	148	74	6	5	326	188	16	3	135	40	4	3	150	44	4	2	68	32	2	8	353	116	10
28	1	50	50	4	2	128	64	6	2	148	74	6	5	326	188	16	3	135	41	4	3	150	44	4	2	69	30	2	8	354	114	10
24	1	40	40	2	2	112	56	4	2	128	64	4	5	280	160	10	3	117	34	4	3	132	38	4	2	62	27	2	8	311	99	10
20	1	36	36	2	2	104	52	4	2	116	58	4	5	256	146	10	3	112	32	4	3	132	38	4	2	58	26	2	8	302	96	10
Sloops	1	32	32	2	2	92	46	4	2	108	54	4	5	232	132	10	3	99	30	4	3	111	32	4	2	48	22	2	8	258	84	10

If more points, rope-bands, or gaskets are used than in the Table, they are made on board.
When sprit-sail courses have cross-reefs, the number of points is twice the number of rope-bands, save 12.
When top-sails have four reefs, let one-third more be added than is allowed in this Table.

PARTICULAR DIRECTIONS
FOR
MAKING EVERY SAIL,
EACH ILLUSTRATED WITH A FIGURE.

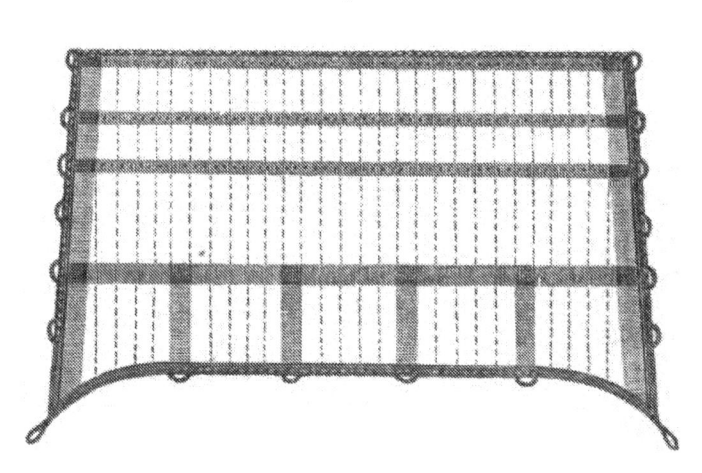

MAIN-COURSE.

This sail is quadrilateral, square on the head, and made of canvas No. 1 or 2. It bends at the head to the main-yard, which hangs to the mast at right angles with the ship's length, and parallel to the deck. It extends within 18 inches of the cleats on the yard-arms, and drops to clear the foot from the boat upon the booms.

GORES. One cloth is gored on each LEECH; and the gore on the FOOT is of one inch per cloth, beginning at two cloths within the nearest buntline cringle, and increasing to the clues. Sometimes, in the merchant-service, two cloths are gored on the leeches, and the gore on the foot is 2 inches per cloth.

For SEAMS, TABLINGS, REEF and HEAD HOLES, consult the general instructions, pages 17—20.

This sail has two REEF-BANDS, of one-third the breadth of a cloth: the upper reef-band is at one-sixth of the depth of the sail from the head, and the lower reef-band is at the same distance from the upper one. The ends go four inches under the leech-linings, which are seamed over them. Ships of forty-four guns and upwards have only one reef-band.

It has also a MIDDLE-BAND, of one breadth of cloth half-way between the lower reef-band and the foot, of the same canvas as the top-lining of the main-top-sail. Middle-bands, in the royal navy, are now formed of half a breadth of canvas, and are simply sewed on at both edges; the sort of canvas is one number less than that the sail is composed of. It is first folded and rubbed down at one third of the breadth; then tabled on the selvage and stuck along the crease; it is then turned down, and tabled and stuck through both the double and single parts with from 68 to 72 stitches per yard. A middle-band is seldom used in the merchant-service.

FOOT-BANDS. In the royal navy this course has now a foot-band, extending from clue to clue, and formed of half a breadth of canvas.

LININGS are of one breadth of cloth from the clue to the earing on the leeches, seamed on and stuck in the middle with from 68 to 72 stitches per yard.

Four BUNTLINE-CLOTHS are placed at equal distances between the leeches, extending from the foot to the lower side of the middle band, which is tabled upon the ends of the buntline-cloths. In the merchant-service, the buntline-cloths run up one-quarter of the depth of the sail, and are two in number only, unless for large vessels: when used, they are generally put on when the sail is half worn.

Two REEF-CRINGLES are made on each leech, one at each reef-band: three BOWLINE-CRINGLES are made at equal distances between the lower reef-cringle and the clue; and BUNTLINE-CRINGLES are made on the foot, one at the end of each buntline-cloth.

In sewing on the bolt-rope, two inches of SLACK-CLOTH are taken up in every cloth, in the head and foot, and one inch and a half in every yard in the leeches.

The MARLING-HOLES extend from the clue to the lower bowline-cringle on the leech, and to the first buntline-cringle at the foot.

The clue is described in the general instructions, page 24.

To find the quantity of canvas, refer to Rule I. page 30.

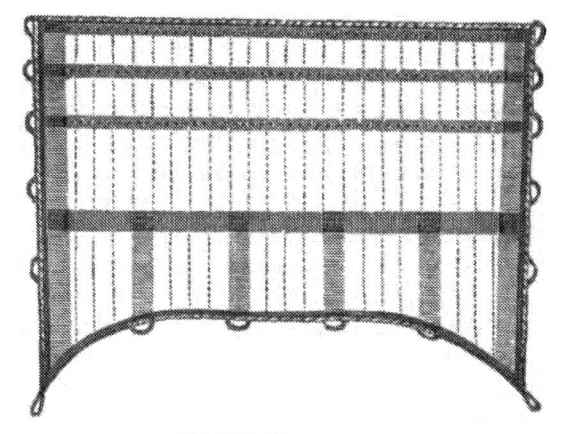

FORE-COURSE.

This sail is quadrilateral, square on the head, and made of canvas No. 1 or 2. It is bent, at the head, to the fore-yard, which hangs to the fore-mast at right angles with the ship's length, and parallel to the deck. It extends within 18 inches of the cleats on the yard-arms, and drops to the main-stay at the foot.

Gores. One cloth is gored on each LEECH, and a gore is made on the FOOT, to drop the clue, 5 to 6 inches per cloth, beginning at two cloths within the nearest buntline-cringle, and increasing to the clues. Sometimes two cloths are gored on each leech, in the merchant-service: and sometimes the foot, with the leeches, are square.

For SEAMS, TABLINGS, REEF and HEAD-HOLES, consult the general instructions, pages 17—19.

Two REEF-BANDS, of one-third the breadth of a cloth, are put on at one-sixth of the depth of the sail asunder, the upper one being at that distance from the head: the ends go four inches under the leech linings, which are sewed over them. Ships of forty-four guns and upwards have only one reef-band.

A MIDDLE-BAND (see Main-Course), of one breadth of cloth, is put on half-way between the lower reef-band and the foot, of the same canvas as the top-lining of the fore-top-sail. It is put on in the same way as that of the main-course. In the merchant-service middle-bands are seldom used.

FOOT-BANDS. See Main-Course.

LININGS on the leeches are of one breadth of cloth, extend

from the clue to the earing, and are put on as those of the main-course.

Four BUNTLINE-CLOTHS, at equal distances between the leeches on the foot, are carried up to the lower side of the middle-band, which is tabled upon the ends of the buntline-cloths. In the merchant-service, the buntline-cloths run up one quarter of the depth of the sail, and are two only in number, unless for large vessels.

Two REEF-CRINGLES are made on the leeches, one at the end of each reef-band; as also are two BOWLINE-CRINGLES; the upper bowline-cringle is made in the middle of the leech, and the lower one equally distant from the upper one and the clue: a BUNTLINE-CRINGLE is also made at the end of each buntline-cloth on the foot. The ends of the buntline-cringles next the clues should be left long enough to be worked under the service, and meet the ends of the clue-rope.

In sewing on the bolt-rope, two inches of SLACK-CLOTH should be taken up in every cloth, in the head and foot, and one inch and a half in every yard in the leeches.

MARLING-HOLES are made in the tabling from the clue to the nearest buntline-cringle on the foot, and one-eighth of the depth of the sail up the leech. They are turned on the contrary side to the roping, in fixing the sail.

The CLUE is described in the general instructions, page 24.

To find the quantity of canvas, refer to Rule I. page 30.

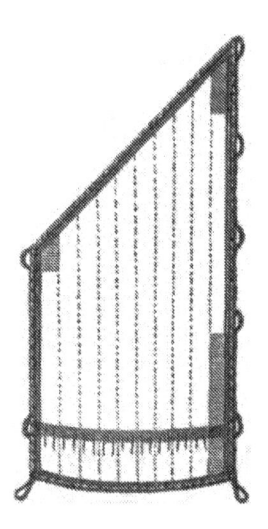

MIZEN-COURSE.

This sail is quadrilateral, and made of canvas No. 2 or 3. The head is bent to the mizen-yard or gaff, and extends within 9 inches of the cleats. The fore-leech is attached to the mizen-mast within 6 or 7 feet of the deck, so that it hangs fore and aft in the plane of the ship's keel. The foot is extended by a sheet to the stern.

Gores. The head is cut with a gore of 16 to 22 inches per cloth, agreeable to the peek: the foot is gored one inch per cloth, leaving two cloths square in the middle. One cloth on the mast-leech is sometimes gored in the navy, and sometimes two cloths in the merchant-service.

For SEAMS, TABLINGS, HEAD-HOLES, and REEF-HANKS, consult the general instructions, pages 17—20, 27.

This sail has a reef-band, 6 or 8 inches broad, at one-fifth of the depth of the mast-leech from the foot.

Lining. The AFTER-LEECH is LINED from the clue with one breadth of cloth 5 yards in length up the leech, and the NOCK and PEEK with pieces so cut from each other that each contains one yard.

One CRINGLE is made on each leech at the ends of the reef-band; and one at the distance of every three-quarters of a yard on the mast-leech, or sometimes holes are worked in the tabling of the mast-leech: a cringle is also made 5 yards from the clue on the after-leech for the throat-brails.

Two inches of SLACK-CLOTH in every yard should be taken up in sewing the bolt-rope on the mast-leech, but none in the foot or after-leech.

The MARLING-HOLES extend two feet each way from the clue.

The CLUE is described in the general instructions, page 24.

To find the quantity of canvas, refer to Rule II. page 31.

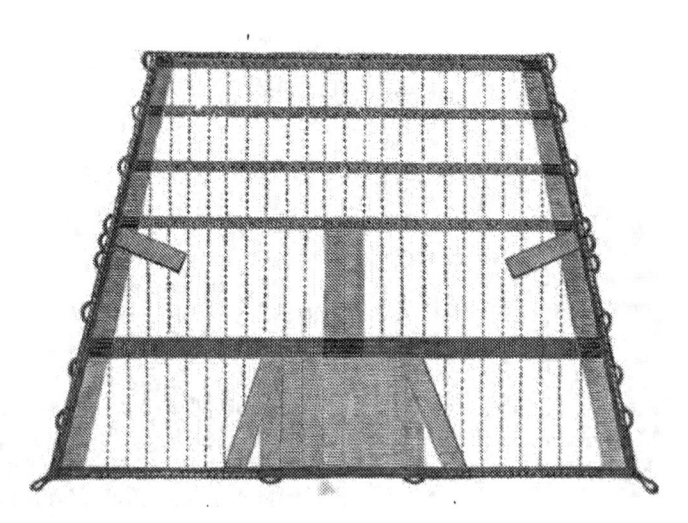

MAIN-TOP-SAIL.

This sail is quadrilateral, square on the head and foot, in the navy, and made of canvas No. 2 or 3, and sometimes 4, or even 5, for small vessels; it is bent at the head to the main-top-sail-yard, which hangs to the main-top-mast at right angles with the ship's length, and parallel to the main-yard: the sail extends within 18 inches of the cleats on the yard-arms, and drops to the main-yard when its own yard is hoisted to the hounds.

GORES. The cloths on the leeches are gored sufficiently for the foot to spread the cleats on the main-yard.

For SEAMS, TABLINGS, REEF and HEAD-HOLES, consult the general instructions, pages 17—20.

This sail has three or four REEF-BANDS, put on at one eighth of the depth of the sail asunder, the upper one being at that distance from the head, and they extend from leech to leech over the linings. They are each half a breadth of canvas put on double; the first side is stuck twice, and the last turned over, so that the reef-holes may be worked upon the double part of the band, which is also stuck with 68 to 72 stitches per yard. Ships above 28 guns have four reef-bands.

A MIDDLE BAND is put on half-way between the lower reef-band and the foot; made and put on in the same way as that of the main-course.

LININGS. The LEECHES are LINED from clue to earing with one cloth, so cut and sewed, as, when put on, to be half a cloth broad at the head, and a cloth and a half broad at the foot; the piece cut out being half the breadth of the cloth at one end, and tapering to a point at the other. This sail has also a TOP-LINING on the aft-side, of canvas No. 5 or 6, which covers one-fifth of the cloths in the foot.

Two MAST-CLOTHS are put on in the middle of the sail, on the aft-side, between the middle-band and lower reef-band.

Two BUNTLINE-CLOTHS are put on the fore-side of the sail, one on each side of the top-lining; their ends are carried up under the middle-band, which is tabled on them. Buntline-cloths, in the royal navy, are now put on in a diagonal direction, agreeable to the figure.

One REEF-CRINGLE is made on the leeches at the end of each reef-band, and a REEF-TACKLE-PENDANT-CRINGLE between the lower reef and upper bowline-cringles: below these are four BOWLINE-CRINGLES; the upper one is on the middle of the leech, and the other three are equally distant from each other between the upper one and the clue. One BUNTLINE-CRINGLE is made in the middle of each buntline-cloth at the foot.

REEF-TACKLE-PIECES. Top-sails have now a reef-tackle-piece at each leech, extending about three cloths on the sail, and pointing directly to the opposite clue, as in the figure.

Three inches of SLACK-CLOTH are taken up in sewing on the bolt-rope in every cloth in the head and foot; 2 inches are allowed for every cloth left open in the top-brim; and one inch and a half is taken up in every yard in the leeches.

The BOLT-ROPE along the top-brim, and for one cloth and a half on each side beyond, is wormed, parcelled, and served, as the clues, and is marled to the sail: but sometimes the whole length of the foot-rope, from clue to clue, is wormed, parcelled, &c. In the royal navy, the latter is now universally the custom.

The MARLING-HOLES extend 3 feet each way from the clue, and along the breadth of the top-lining at the top-brim.

The CLUE is described in the general instructions, page 24.

In the MERCHANT-SERVICE, the reef-bands are farther distant from each other: the foot is gored from 2 to 4 inches per cloth, one-third of the breadth of the foot from the clues; the leech-linings are but 9 inches broad at the head, and 15 inches broad at the foot; the top-lining and buntline-cloths cover one-third of the cloths in the foot, and are carried up one-third of the depth of the sail; the buntline-cloths are half a yard shorter than the top-lining, and the leeches have only three bowline-cringles.

To find the quantity of canvas, refer to Rule I. page 30.

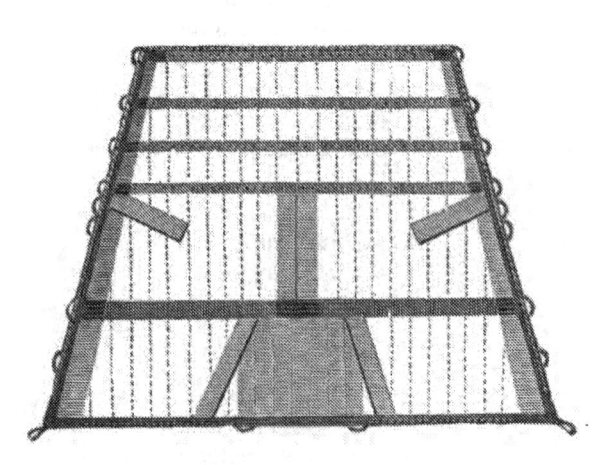

FORE-TOP-SAIL.

This sail is quadrilateral, square on the head and foot in the royal navy, and made of canvas No. 2 or 3, of sometimes 4, or even 5, for small vessels. The head is bent to the fore-top-sail-yard, and it hangs to the fore-mast at right angles with the ship's length, and parallel to the fore-yard, extending, at the head, within 18 inches of the cleats on the yard-arms.

GORES. The cloths on each leech are gored sufficiently for the foot to spread the length of the fore-yard. Sometimes, in the merchant-service, the foot is gored 2 to 4 inches per cloth, from one-third of the breadth of the foot to the clues.

For SEAMS, TABLINGS, REEF, and HEAD-HOLES, consult the general instructions, pages 17—19.

One REEF-CRINGLE is made at the end of each reef-band, and a REEF-PENDANT-CRINGLE between the lower reef and upper bowline cringles. The reef and reef-pendant-cringles are stuck through holes made in the tabling; and beneath them are made three BOWLINE-CRINGLES; the upper one upon the middle of the leech, and the others equally asunder between that and the clue: two BUNTLINE-CRINGLES are also made, one in the middle of each buntline-cloth on the foot.

REEF-TACKLE-PIECES, as main-top-sail.

The LININGS, MAST-CLOTHS, MIDDLE and REEF BANDS, CLUES, &c. are the same as for the main-top-sail, page 44.

SLACK-CLOTH, BOLT-ROPE, and MARLING-HOLES, as main-top-sail.

To find the quantity of canvas, refer to Rule I. page 30.

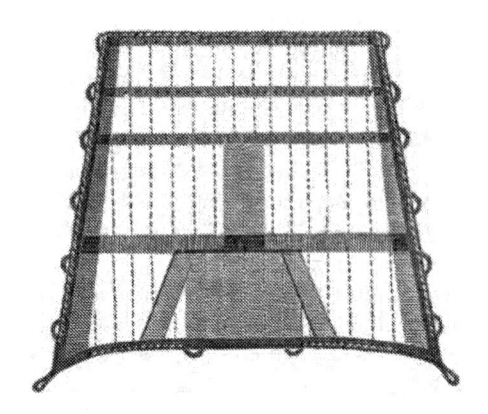

MIZEN-TOP-SAIL.

This sail is quadrilateral, square on the head, and made of canvas No. 4, 5, or 6: it is bent at the head to the mizen-top-sail yard, and hangs to the mizen-top-mast at right angles, with the ship's length, and parallel to the cross-jack-yard, extending within 12 inches of the cleats on the yard-arms.

GORES. The cloths on the leeches are gored sufficiently for the foot to spread the length of the cross-jack-yard, and the clues reach the sheet-blocks on the cross-jack-yard-arms, when both yards are hoisted. The gore on the foot is three-quarters of a yard deep, and begins at two cloths from the buntline-cringle, on the side next the clues. In the merchant-service, the foot is sometimes square.

For SEAMS, TABLINGS, REEF and HEAD-HOLES, consult the general instructions, pages 17—19.

Mizen-top-sails, for 50-gun ships and upwards, have three REEF-BANDS at one-eighth of the depth of the sail asunder from the head; and for 44-gun ships and under, two reef-bands, one-seventh of the depth of the sail asunder, put on as those of the main-top-sail. In the merchant-service, they have two reefs, as the 44-gun ship, but no middle-band.

A MIDDLE-BAND, of one breadth of cloth, the same as the main-top-sail, is put on half-way between the lower reef-band and the foot.

The LEECHES are LINED with one breadth of cloth, as the main-top-sail. In the merchant-service, they are lined with part of a cloth, 9 inches broad at the head, and 15 inches at the foot.

The TOP-LINING is put on the aft-side, and covers one-fifth of the cloths in the foot, as the main and fore-top-sails. In the merchant-service, the top-lining covers one-third of the cloths in the foot, and is carried up one-third of the depth of the sail, and the buntline-cloths are half a yard shorter than the top-lining.

The BUNTLINE-CLOTHS are on the fore-side, and are carried under the middle-band, as the main and fore top-sails.

One inch and a half of SLACK-CLOTH is taken up, in sewing on the bolt-rope, in every yard in the leeches, three inches in every cloth in the head and foot, and two inches are allowed for every cloth in the top-brim.

One REEF-CRINGLE is made on the leeches at the end of each reef-band, and three BOWLINE-CRINGLES are made on each leech, the upper one in the middle of the leech, and the others equally distant between that and the clue. Forty-four-gun ships and upwards have a REEF-PENDANT-CRINGLE between the lower reef and upper bowline-cringles, and, of course, REEF-TACKLE-PIECES as the main-top-sail.

The BOLT-ROPE that comes abreast the top-brim is wormed, parcelled, served, and marled, as the main-top-sails.

The CLUES are described in the general instructions, page 24.

To find the quantity of canvas, refer to Rule I. page 30.

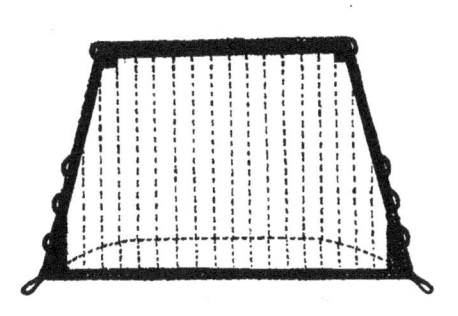

MAIN-TOP-GALLANT-SAIL.

This sail is quadrilateral, and square on the head and foot, in the navy, and made of canvas No. 6 or 7; the head is bent to the

the length of the mizen-top-sail-yard. In the merchant-service, a small gore is sometimes made on the foot, beginning at one-third of the breadth from the clue. The foot-gores, in the royal navy, as the main-top-gallant-sail.

The PIECES at the clues and earings are each a quarter of a yard in length.

For the SEAMS, TABLINGS, HEAD-HOLES, and CLUES, consult the general instructions, pages 17—19, and 25.

SLACK-CLOTH the same as the main-top-gallant-sail.

To find the quantity of canvas, refer to Rule I. page 30.

MAIN-ROYAL.

This sail is quadrilateral, square on the head and foot, and made of canvas No. 8. The head is bent to the main-royal-yard, which hangs to the main-top-gallant-royal-mast-head, at right angles with the ship's length, and parallel with the main-top gallant-yard, extending within 4 inches of the cleats on the yard-arms.

GORES. The cloths on the leeches are gored sufficiently for the foot to spread the length of the main-top-gallant-yard, and it drops for the clues to reach to the main-top-gallant-yard-arms, when both yards are hoisted.

For SEAMS, TABLINGS, HEAD-HOLES, and CLUES, consult the general instructions, pages 17—19, and 25.

To find the quantity of canvas, refer to Rule I. page 30.

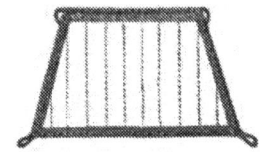

FORE-ROYAL.

This sail is quadrilateral, square on the head and foot, and made of canvas No. 8. The head is bent to the fore-royal-yard, which hangs to the fore-top-gallant-royal-mast-head, at right angles with the ship's length, and parallel with the fore-top-gallant-yard, extending within 4 inches of the cleats on the yard-arms.

GORES. The cloths are gored on the leeches sufficiently for the foot to spread the length of the fore-top-gallant-yard, and it drops for the clues to reach the fore-top-gallant-yard-arms, when both yards are hoisted.

For SEAMS, TABLINGS, HEAD-HOLES, and CLUES, consult the general instructions, pages 17—19, and 25.

To find the quantity of canvas, refer to Rule I. page 30.

MIZEN-ROYAL.

This sail is quadrilateral, square on the head and foot, and made of canvas No. 8. The head is bent to the mizen-royal-yard, which hangs to the head of the mizen-top-gallant-royal-mast, at right angles with the ship's length, and parallel with the mizen-top-gallant-yard, extending within four inches of the cleats on the yard-arms. It is a sail very seldom used.

GORES. The cloths are gored on each leech sufficiently for the foot to spread the mizen-top-gallant-yard, and it drops for the clues to reach to the mizen-top-gallant-yard-arms, when both yards are hoisted.

For SEAMS, TABLINGS, HEAD-HOLES, and CLUES, consult the general instructions, pages 17—19, and 25.

To find the quantity of canvas, refer to Rule I. page 30.

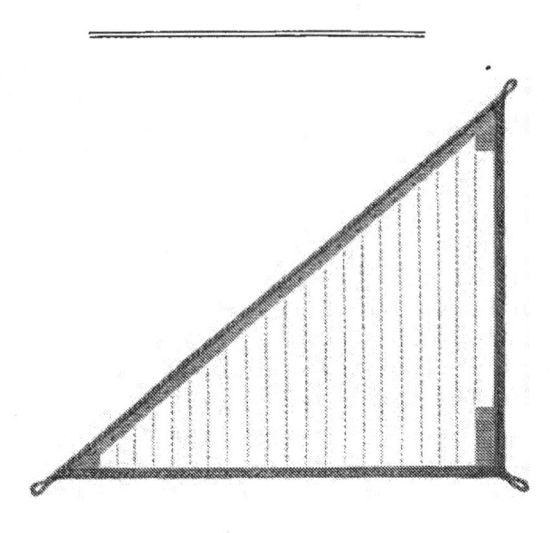

MAIN-STAY-SAIL.

This sail is triangular, square on the foot in the royal navy, and made of canvas No. 1 to 3. It is extended upon the main-stay-sail-stay, between the main and fore masts, so that the foot will clear the boat upon the booms. This sail is seldom used in large vessels.

A regular GORE is made on the stay of 17 to 19 inches per cloth.

The cloth at the tack is so cut as to fall to the foot and form its own LINING. The CLUE-PIECE extends two yards up the leech, and the PEEK-PIECE is one yard in length.

For SEAMS and TABLINGS, consult the general instructions, pages 17 and 18.

HOLES are made on the STAY, 27 inches asunder; generally

one hole is made at every seam; and MARLING-HOLES are made 2 feet each way from the clue.

In sewing on the bolt-rope, 3 inches SLACK should be taken up in every yard in the stay, and one inch in every cloth in the foot, but none in the leech.

IRON THIMBLES are sometimes stuck at the tack and peek, but when none, the tack and peek are the same as the clue.

The CLUE is described in the general instructions, page 25.

A CRINGLE is made on the leech for the brails; but is usually done by the seamen on board.

In the merchant-service, this sail is frequently cut with a bunt, and a gore is sometimes made on the foot, with a sweep. It also frequently has a reef-band at about 4 feet from the foot, and sometimes a bonnet.

To find the quantity of canvas, refer to Rule III. page 32.

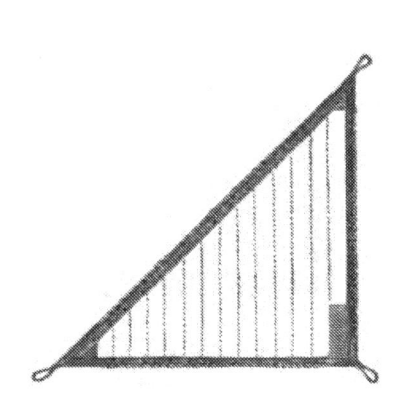

FORE-STAY-SAIL.

This sail is triangular, square on the foot, and made of canvas No. 1 to 3. It is extended on the fore-stay, between the fore-mast and bow-sprit.

A regular GORE is made on the stay, of 21 to 23 inches per cloth.

The cloth at the tack is so cut as to fall to the foot, and form its own LINING: the CLUE-PIECE extends two yards up the leech, and the PEEK-PIECE is half a yard in length.

For SEAMS and TABLINGS consult the general instructions, pages 17 and 18.

The HOLES on the STAY are 27 inches asunder; generally one hole is made at every seam; and the MARLING-HOLES extend 2 feet each way from the clue.

Three inches SLACK should be taken up in every yard in the stay when sewing on the bolt-rope, and one inch in every cloth in the foot, but none in the leech.

THIMBLES are sometimes stuck at the tack and peek, but when none, the tack and peek are the same as the clue.

The clue is described in the general instructions, page 25.

To find the quantity of canvas, refer to Rule III. page 32.

MIZEN-STAY-SAIL.

This sail is quadrilateral, square on the foot, and made of canvas No. 2 or 3. It has a bunt, or fore-leech, three-fifths of the depth of the after-leech, in the navy, and one-third or one-fourth of the depth of the after-leech in the merchant-service; and it is extended on the mizen-stay, between the main and mizen-masts. The foot drops within 6 or 7 feet of the quarter-deck.

GORES. Two cloths are generally gored on the bunt; and the stay is gored from 10 to 12 inches per cloth. If the depth of the bunt be subtracted from the depth of the leech, the remainder, divided by the number of gored cloths, gives the depth of each gore on the stay.

For SEAMS and TABLINGS, consult the general instructions, pages 17 and 18.

The bunt or fore-leech is LINED with half a breadth of cloth; the CLUE-PIECE is two yards long, and the PEEK-PIECE one yard. In the merchant-service, the tack, peek, and nock-pieces, are generally but three-quarters of a yard in length.

One or two CRINGLES are made on the after-leech for the brails, and thimbles are stuck in the middle of the sail, to lead them fair through; but this is usually done by the seamen on board.

HOLES are made on the stay, three-quarters of a yard asunder; generally one hole is made to every seam, and MARLING-HOLES two feet each way from the clue.

Three inches of SLACK-CLOTH should be taken in with the rope in every yard in the stay, and one inch in every cloth in the foot, but none in the leech.

THIMBLES are sometimes stuck at the tack and peek; but, when thimbles are not used, the tack and peek are frequently marled as the clue.

The CLUE is described in the general instructions, page 25.

To find the quantity of canvas, refer to Rule IV. page 33.

56   THE PRACTICE OF SAIL-MAKING.

For **SEAMS** and **TABLINGS** consult the general instructions, pages 17 and 18.

The **HOLES** on the **STAY** are 27 inches asunder; generally one hole is made at every seam; and the **MARLING-HOLES** extend 2 feet each way from the clue.

Three inches **SLACK** should be taken up in every yard in the stay when sewing on the bolt-rope, and one inch in every cloth in the foot, but none in the leech.

THIMBLES are sometimes stuck at the tack and peek, but when none, the tack and peek are the same as the clue.

The clue is described in the general instructions, page 25.

To find the quantity of canvas, refer to Rule III. page 32.

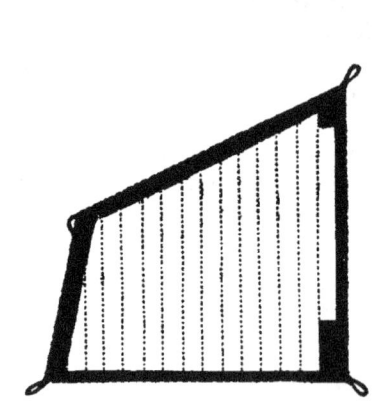

MIZEN-STAY-SAIL.

This sail is quadrilateral, square on the foot, and made of canvas No. 2 or 3. It has a bunt, or fore-leech, three-fifths of the depth of the after-leech, in the navy, and one-third or one-fourth of the depth of the after-leech in the merchant-service; and it is extended on the mizen-stay, between the main and mizen-masts. The foot drops within 6 or 7 feet of the quarter-deck.

GORES. Two cloths are generally gored on the bunt; and the stay is gored from 10 to 12 inches per cloth. If the depth of the bunt be subtracted from the depth of the leech, the remainder divided by the number of gored cloths will give the depth of the gore on the stay.

For SEAMS and TABLINGS, consult the general instructions, pages 17 and 18.

The bunt or fore-leech is LINED with half a breadth of cloth; the CLUE-PIECE is two yards long, and the PEEK-PIECE one yard. In the merchant-service, the tack, peek, and nock-pieces, are generally but three-quarters of a yard in length.

One or two CRINGLES are made on the after-leech for the brails, and thimbles are stuck in the middle of the sail, to lead them fair through; but this is usually done by the seamen on board.

HOLES are made on the stay, three-quarters of a yard asunder; generally one hole is made to every seam, and MARLING-HOLES two feet each way from the clue.

Three inches of SLACK-CLOTH should be taken in with the rope in every yard in the stay, and one inch in every cloth in the foot, but none in the leech.

THIMBLES are sometimes stuck at the tack and peek; but, when thimbles are not used, the tack and peek are frequently marled as the clue.

The CLUE is described in the general instructions, page 25.

To find the quantity of canvas, refer to Rule IV. page 33.

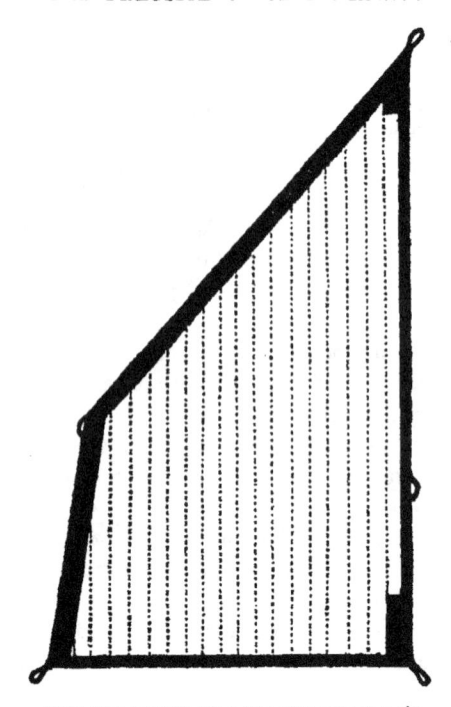

MAIN-TOP-MAST-STAY-SAIL.

This sail is quadrilateral, cut square on the foot, and made of canvas No. 5 or 6. It is extended on the main-top-mast-preventer-stay, between the main and fore-top-masts. The leech is 4 or 5 yards deeper than the main-top-sail, and there are one or two cloths more in the foot than the leech is yards in depth.

In large merchant-ships the leech is 4 or 5 yards deeper than the main-top-sail; but in smaller ships, only one or two yards; and there are from one to three cloths more in the foot than the leech is yards in depth.

The bunt is two-fifths of the depth of the leech: but in the merchant-service it is from two-fifths to one-half of the depth.

GORES. Two cloths are generally gored on the bunt, and the stay is gored 22 inches per cloth. If the depth at the nock-seam be subtracted from the depth of the leech, the remainder, divided by the number of gored cloths, gives the depth of each gore on the stay.

For SEAMS and TABLINGS, consult the general instructions, pages 17 and 18.

THE PRACTICE OF SAIL-MAKING. 59

The bunt is lined with half a breadth of cloth. The CLUE-PIECE is two yards long, and the PEEK-PIECE one yard. In the merchant-service, this sail generally has tack, nock, and peek-pieces, each three-quarters of a yard in length.

One or two CRINGLES are made on the after-leech for the brails, and thimbles are stuck in the middle of the sails, to lead them fair through; but this is usually done by the seamen on board.

The HOLES on the stay are 27 inches asunder; generally one hole is made at every seam; and MARLING-HOLES are made two feet each way from the clue.

Three inches of SLACK-CLOTH should be taken up in every yard in the stay, and one inch in every cloth in the foot, but none in the leech.

THIMBLES are sometimes stuck in the tack and peek; when there are none, the tack and peek are the same as the clue, and are fixed or marled on.

The CLUE is described in the general instructions, page 25.

To find the quantity of canvas, refer to Rule IV. page 33.

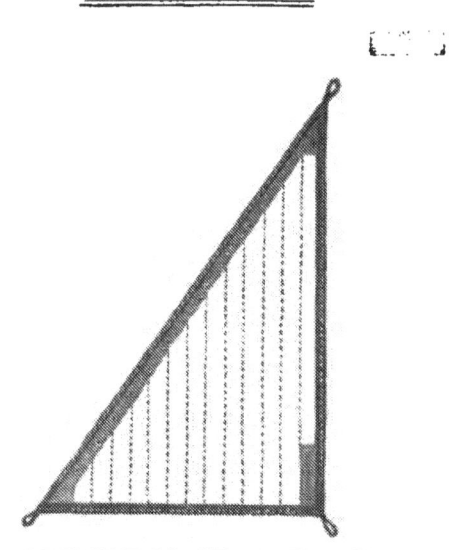

FORE-TOP-MAST-STAY-SAIL.

This sail is triangular, cut square on the foot, and made of canvas No. 5, 6, or 7, in the royal navy; and of canvas No. 1,

2, or 3, in the merchant-service. It is extended on the fore-topmast-stay-sail-stay, and the foot is spread on the bowsprit. The leech is of the same depth as the fore-top-sail; and 2 or 3 cloths are allowed in the foot for every yard in the depth of the leech. In the merchant-service, one cloth only is allowed in the foot for every yard in the depth of the leech.

GORES. The stay is gored 30 inches per cloth. The depth of the gore on each cloth in the stay is found by dividing the depth of the leech by the number of cloths. In the merchant-service, the foot is gored from the clue to the tack, corresponding with the direction of the bowsprit.

For SEAMS and TABLINGS, consult the general instructions, pages 17 and 18.

The cloth at the tack is so cut as to fall to the foot, and form its own LINING. The CLUE-PIECE is two yards long, and the PEEK-PIECE one yard. In the merchant-service, the piece at the clue is in general but one yard in length, and the tack and peek-pieces half a yard each.

The HOLES on the stay are 27 inches asunder, and the MARLING-HOLES extend two feet each way from the clue.

Three inches SLACK should be taken up in sewing on the rope, in every yard in the stay, and one inch in every cloth in the foot, but none in the leech.

THIMBLES are sometimes stuck at the tack and peek; when there are none, the tack and peek are the same as the clue, and are fixed or marled on.

The CLUE is seized with small line, and is described in the general instructions, page 25.

To find the quantity of canvas, refer to Rule III. page 32.

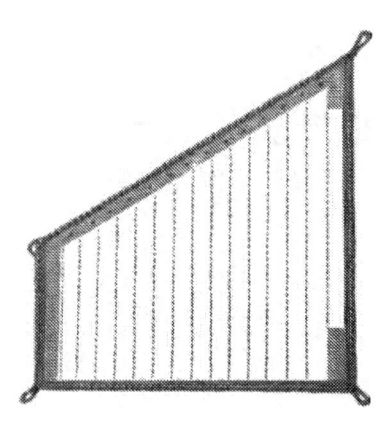

MIDDLE-STAY-SAIL.

This sail is quadrilateral, cut square on the foot, and made of canvas No. 6 or 7. It has a square bunt, or fore-leech, five-twelfths of the depth of the after-leech, and it is extended on the middle-stay-sail-stay, between the main-top-mast-stay and main-top-gallant-stay.

The leech is from 4 to 7 yards deeper than the main-top-gallant-sail, and there are from 6 to 8 cloths more in the foot than the leech is yards in depth. Sloops and brigs in the navy have only from one to three cloths more in the foot than yards in the depth of the leech.

In the merchant-service, the leech is sometimes of the same depth as the main-top-gallant-sail, but, generally, one, two, or three yards more; and the sail has from 5 to 10 cloths more in the foot than yards in the depth of the leech.

GORES. The stay is gored 13 inches and a half per cloth. If the depth of the bunt be subtracted from the depth of the leech, the remainder, divided by the number of cloths, gives the depth of each gore on the stay.

For SEAMS and TABLINGS, consult the general instructions, pages 17 and 18.

The bunt is LINED with half a breadth of cloth, the CLUE with a piece two yards long, and the PEEK with a piece one yard in length.

THE PRACTICE OF SAIL-MAKING.

Three inches of SLACK-CLOTH should be taken up in every yard in the stay, when sewing on the rope, and one inch in every cloth in the foot, but none in the leech.

THIMBLES are sometimes stuck at the tack and peek; when there are none, the tack and peek are the same as the clue, and are marled on.

The CLUE is described in the general instructions, page 25.

To find the quantity of canvas, refer to Rule V. page 34.

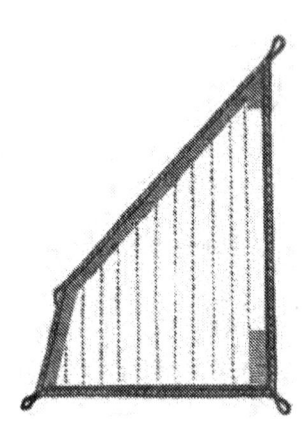

MIZEN-TOP-MAST-STAY-SAIL.

This sail is quadrilateral, cut square on the foot, and made of canvas No. 7. It has a bunt, or fore-leech, three-sevenths or one-third of the depth of the after-leech, and is extended on the mizen-top-mast-stay, between the main and mizen-top-masts.

The leech is one or two yards deeper than the mizen-top-sail, and there are from 2 to 5 cloths more in the foot than the leech is yards in depth.

One cloth is generally gored on the bunt, and the stay is gored twenty-four inches per cloth. If the length of the nock-seam be subtracted from the depth of the leech, the remainder, divided by the number of cloths in the stay, gives the depth of each gore.

For SEAMS and TABLINGS, consult the general instructions, pages 17 and 18.

The bunt is LINED with half a breadth of cloth: the CLUE-PIECE is two yards long, and the PEEK-PIECE one yard. In the merchant-service, the clue-piece is generally one yard long, and the peek-piece half a yard.

Three inches SLACK should be taken up in every yard in the stay, and one inch in every cloth in the foot, but none in the leech.

THIMBLES are generally stuck in the tack and peek; but, when no thimbles, the tack and peek are the same as the clue.

The CLUE is described in the general instructions, page 25.

To find the quantity of canvas, refer to Rule IV. page 33.

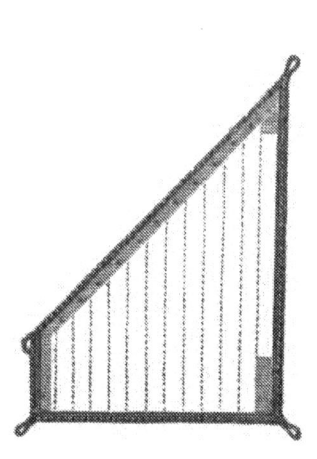

MAIN-TOP-GALLANT-STAY-SAIL.

This sail is quadrilateral, cut square on the foot, and made of canvas No. 7. It has a bunt from one-third to three-sevenths of the depth of the leech, and is extended on the main-top-gallant-stay-sail-stay between the main and the fore-top-gallant-masts.

The leech is nearly of the same depth as the leech of the middle-stay-sail, and there are from 3 to 6 cloths more in the foot than the leech is yards in depth. In the merchant-service, there are from 2 to 8 cloths more in the foot than the leech is yards in depth.

The stay is GORED 24 inches per cloth. If the depth of the bunt be subtracted from the depth of the leech, the remainder, divided by the number of cloths, gives the depth of the gore on each cloth.

For SEAMS and TABLINGS, consult the general instructions, pages 17 and 18.

The bunt is LINED with half a breadth of cloth, the CLUE-PIECE is two yards long, and the PEEK-PIECE one yard. In the merchant-service, the clue-piece is only one yard; and the tack, nock, and peek-pieces, are each half a yard in length.

The HOLES on the stay are 27 inches asunder.

In sewing on the bolt-rope, three inches SLACK should be taken up in every yard in the stay, and one inch in every cloth in the foot, but none in the leech.

THIMBLES are generally stuck at the tack, nock, and peek. When there are no thimbles, the tack and peek are the same as the clue.

The CLUE is described in the general instructions, page 25.

To find the quantity of canvas, refer to Rule V. page 34.

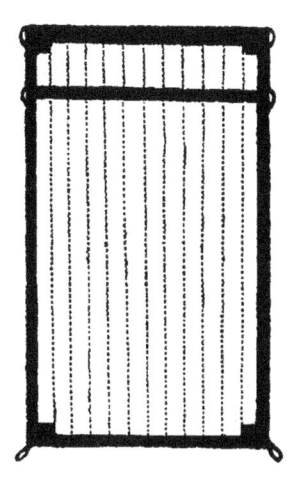

LOWER-MAIN-STUDDING-SAILS.

These sails are quadrilateral, cut square on the head, foot, and leeches, and made of canvas No. 6 or 7. They spread beyond the leeches of the main-course, the heads being bent to the main-studding-sail-yards, and the feet extended on the boom.

The sails are 2 or 3 yards deeper than the main-course. In large ships, two cloths more, and in small ships, one cloth less, are allowed, for the breadth, than the number of yards in the depth. In the royal navy, studding-sails are now made much broader: see Table. But in the merchant-service, they are only one yard deeper, or of the same depth as the main-course; and from 2 to 7 cloths are allowed in the foot more than the number of yards in the depth.

For SEAMS, TABLINGS, REEF and HEAD-HOLES, consult the general instructions, pages 17—20.

A REEF-BAND, 6 inches wide, is put on at one-eighth of the depth from the head, and PIECES of one-quarter or half a yard in length, are sometimes put on at the CLUES and EARINGS.

One inch of SLACK-CLOTH should be taken up, in sewing on the bolt-rope, in every cloth in the foot. The rope should be sewed home to the clue, and a REEF-CRINGLE made at each end of the reef-band.

The CLUES are described in the general instructions, page 25.

To find the quantity of canvas, refer to Rule VI. page 34.

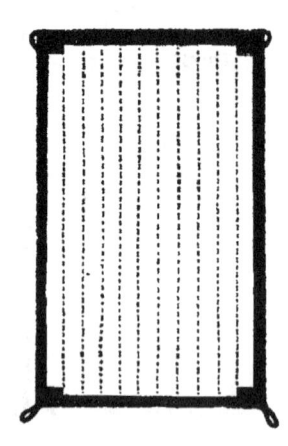

LOWER-FORE-STUDDING-SAILS.

These sails are quadrilateral, square on the head, foot, and leeches, and made of canvas No. 6 or 7. They are spread beyond the leeches of the fore-course, the heads being bent to the fore-studding-sail-yards, and the feet extended on the boom.

The depth is the same as the main-course, or from one to two yards more, and the breadth is one cloth less than the main-studding-sail.

For SEAMS, TABLINGS, and HEAD-HOLES, consult the general instructions, pages 17—20.

One quarter or half a yard of cloth is sometimes put on as a LINING at the clues and earings.

One inch of SLACK-CLOTH should be taken up in every cloth in the foot, when sewing on the bolt-rope, which is to be sewed home to the clues.

The CLUES are described in the general instructions, page 25.

To find the quantity of canvas, refer to Rule VI. page 34.

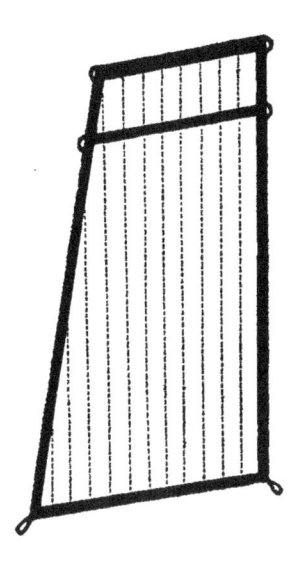

MAIN-TOP-MAST-STUDDING-SAILS.

These sails are quadrilateral, and made of canvas No. 6 or 7. They are spread beyond the leeches of the main-top-sail, the heads being bent to their respective yards, and the feet extended on the boom.

The depth is one yard more than the main-top-sail, and two cloths less are allowed for the breadth of the foot than the number of yards in the depth of the leech.

GORES. Four cloths are gored on the outer leech, in the navy, and from 4 to 7 cloths in the merchant-service; and a regular gore is made on the head and foot of 4 inches per cloth, decreasing to the outer earing at the head, and increasing to the tack or outer clue at the foot.

For SEAMS, TABLINGS, REEF and HEAD-HOLES, consult the general instructions, pages 17—20.

A REEF-BAND, 6 inches broad, is put on at one-eighth of the depth of the sail from the head.

One inch and a half SLACK-CLOTH should be taken up in every yard in the gored leech, when sewing on the bolt-rope, and one inch in every cloth in the foot, but none in the square leech. The rope is to be sewed home to the clues.

One REEF-CRINGLE is made on the leeches at each end of the reef-band, and a DOWNHAUL-CRINGLE is made on the outer leech, about half the depth of the leech from the head.

The CLUES are described in the general instructions, page 25.

To find the quantity of canvas, refer to Rule I. page 30.

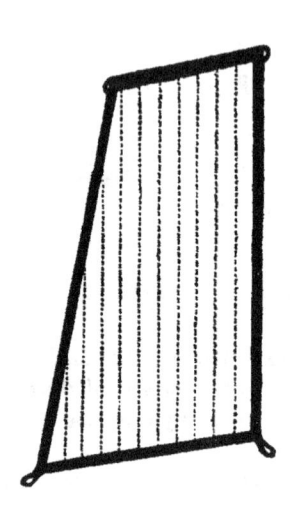

FORE-TOP-MAST-STUDDING-SAILS.

These sails are quadrilateral, and made of canvas No. 6 or 7. They are spread beyond the leeches of the fore-top-sail, the heads being bent to their respective yards, and the feet extended on the boom.

The depth is one yard more than the fore-top-sail, and one cloth less is allowed for the breadth of the foot than in the main-top-mast-studding-sail.

GORES. Four cloths are gored on the outer leech, in the navy, and from 4 to 7 cloths, in the merchant-service; and a regular gore is made on the head and foot of 4 inches per cloth, decreasing to the outer earing at the head, and increasing to the tack or outer clue at the foot.

For SEAMS, TABLINGS, and HEAD-HOLES, consult the general instructions, pages 17—20.

One inch and a half SLACK-CLOTH should be taken up in every yard in the gored leech, when sewing on the rope, and one inch in every cloth in the foot, but none in the square leech. The rope is to be sewed home to the clues.

A DOWNHAUL-CRINGLE is made on the outer leech at about half the depth of the sail from the head.

The CLUES are described in the general instructions, page 25.

To find the quantity of canvas, refer to Rule I. page 30.

MAIN-TOP-GALLANT-STUDDING-SAILS.

These sails are quadrilateral, and made of canvas No. 7 or 8. They are spread beyond the leeches of the main-top-gallant-sail, the heads being bent to their respective yards, and the feet extended on the boom.

The depth is half a yard more than the main-top-gallant-sail. In large ships there are 5 cloths more allowed for the breadth of the foot than the number of yards in the depth, but in small ships there are only 3 more, or the same number of cloths in the breadth of the foot as yards in the depth of the leech.

GORES. The outer leech is gored from two to four cloths, and an even gore is made on the head and foot from 3 to 5 inches per cloth, decreasing to the outer earing at the head, and increasing to the tack at the foot.

For SEAMS, TABLINGS, and HEAD-HOLES, consult the general instructions, pages 17—20.

One inch and a half of SLACK-CLOTH should be taken up in every yard, when sewing the bolt-rope on the gored leech, and one inch in every cloth in the foot, but none in the square leech.

The CLUES are described in the general instructions, page 25.

To find the quantity of canvas, refer to Rule I. page 30.

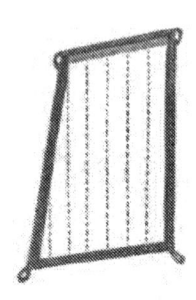

FORE-TOP-GALLANT-STUDDING-SAILS.

These sails are quadrilateral, and made of canvas No. 7 or 8. They are spread beyond the leeches of the fore-top-gallant-sail, the heads being bent to their respective yards, and the feet extended on the boom.

The depth is half a yard more than the fore-top-gallant-sail. In large ships there are 5 cloths more allowed for the breadth of the foot than the number of yards in the depth, but in small ships there are only 3 more, or the same number of cloths in the foot as yards in the depth of the leech.

GORES. The outer leech is gored from 2 to 4 cloths, and an even gore is made on the head and foot from 3 to 5 inches per cloth, decreasing to the outer earing at the head, and increasing to the tack at the foot.

For SEAMS, TABLINGS, and HEAD-HOLES, consult the general instructions, pages 17—20.

Once inch and a half of SLACK-CLOTH should be taken up in every yard in the gored leech, when sewing on the rope, and one inch in every yard in the foot, but none in the square leech.

The CLUES are described in the general instructions, page 25.

To find the quantity of canvas, refer to Rule I. page 30.

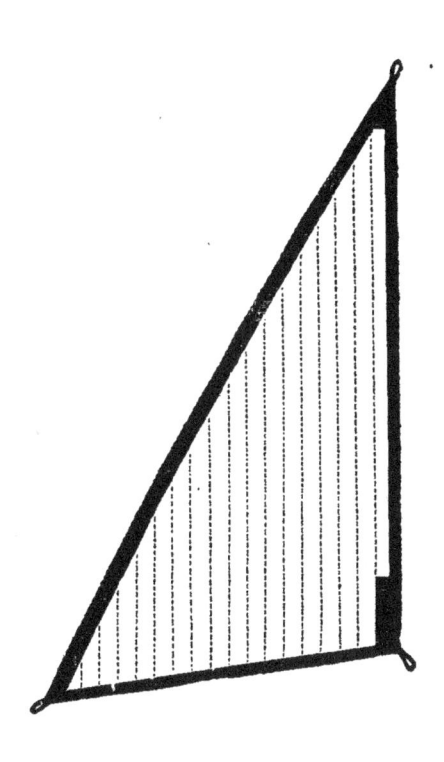

JIB.

This sail is triangular, and made of canvas No. 6 or 7. It is the foremost sail of a ship, and differs in shape but little from a stay-sail. The foot is extended from the outer end of the bowsprit by the jib-boom, and it slides on the jib-stay, which is attached to the fore-top-mast-head. The leech is about twice the depth of the leech of the fore-stay-sail, and one cloth more is allowed for the breadth of the foot, than the leech is yards in depth.

GORES. The stay is cut with a small curve, or roach. The length of the regular gore per cloth may be found by dividing the depth of the stay by the number of cloths. The gores should be allowed full, and the curve cut fair after the sail is sewed together; which, it is supposed, makes it set better when bent.

The foot has an even gore of three inches per cloth, decreasing from the tack to the clue, which is governed by the stive of the bowsprit. For brigs, this sail has a circular foot, and sometimes for ships, in the merchant-service. The seams are generally one inch broader at the foot than at the head, when cut with a circular or roach foot.

For SEAMS and TABLINGS, consult the general instructions, pages 17 and 18.

The CLUE-PIECE is two yards, and the PEEK-PIECE is one yard long, and the cloth at the tack is so cut as to fall to the foot, and form its own LINING.

MARLING-HOLES are made two feet each way from the clue, and one hole is made in every yard in the stay.

In sewing on the bolt-rope, four or five inches of SLACK-CLOTH should be taken up in every yard in the stay, one inch in every cloth in the foot, and none on the leech.

IRON THIMBLES are sometimes seized on at the tack and peek, but, when thimbles are not used, the tack and peek are the same as the clue, and are frequently marled on.

The CLUE is made with clue-rope, exactly like the clues of lower stay-sails, as described in the general instructions, page 25.

To find the quantity of canvas, refer to Rule III. page 32.

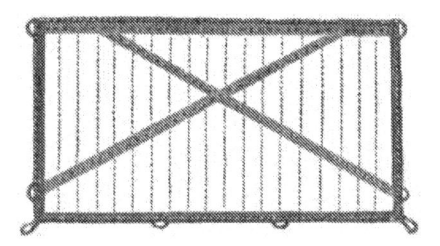

SPRIT-SAIL-COURSE.

This sail is quadrilateral, square on the head, foot, and leeches, and made of canvas No. 2 or 3. It is bent at the head to the sprit-sail-yard, and hangs under the bowsprit at right angles with the ship's length, extending within 9 inches of the cleats on the yard-arms.

For SEAMS, TABLINGS, REEF and HEAD-HOLES, consult the general instructions, pages 17—20.

Two REEF-BANDS, one-third of the breadth of a cloth, are put on diagonally; the ends on the leeches being 27 inches from the clues, and those at the head on the first or second seam from the earings. In the royal navy the cross-reefs are now entirely obsolete. Sometimes a reef-band is put on from leech to leech, at one-fifth of the depth of the sail from the head.

A WATER-HOLE, from 4 to 6 inches diameter, is made in the second cloth from each leech, near the foot, or opposite the reef-cringles. The water-holes are also obsolete. The MARLING-HOLES extend to two feet each way from the clues.

The CLUES are described in the general instructions, page 25.

A REEF-CRINGLE is made on the leeches at the end of each reef-band, and two BUNTLINE-CRINGLES are made on the foot-rope, at one-third of the breadth of the foot from each clue.

No SLACK-CLOTH is taken up in sewing on the bolt-rope.

To find the quantity of canvas, refer to Rule VI. page 34.

SPRIT-SAIL-TOP-SAIL.

This sail is quadrilateral, cut square on the head and foot, and made of canvas No. 6 or 7. The head is bent to the sprit-sail-top-sail-yard, which hangs under the jib-boom, at right angles with the ship's length, and the foot is spread on the sprit-sail-yard. It has as many cloths in the head as the fore-top-gallant-sail; and is of the same depth as the main-top-gallant-sail, in the navy, but from one to two feet deeper in the merchant-service.

GORES. The leeches are gored from 4 to 5 cloths, sufficiently for the foot to spread to the cleats on the outer ends of the sprit-sail-yard.

For SEAMS, TABLINGS, and HEAD-HOLES, consult the general instructions, pages 17—20.

Two inches of SLACK-CLOTH should be taken up in every cloth in the foot when sewing on the bolt-rope, and one inch in every yard in the leeches.

The CLUES are described in the general instructions, page 25.

To find the quantity of canvas, refer to Rule I. page 30.

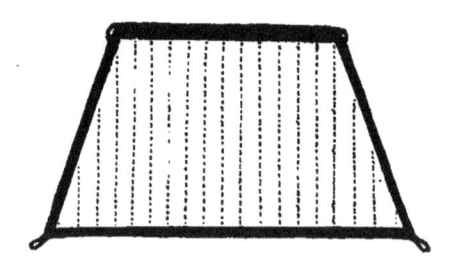

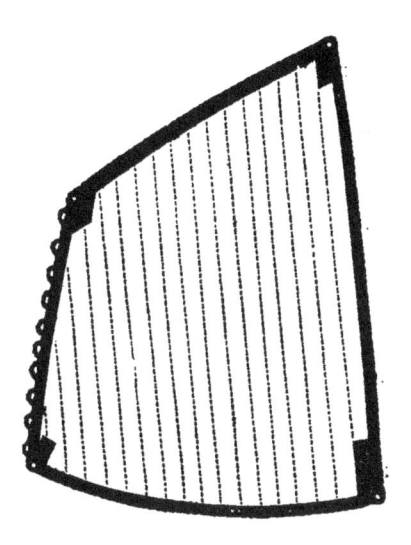

DRIVER-BOOM-SAIL.

This sail is quadrilateral, and made of canvas No. 5 or 6, and is occasionally hoisted to the mizen-yard or gaff, in light fair winds. The fore-leech is attached to the mizen-mast, and the head to the mizen-yard or gaff: the foot is extended by the boom which hangs fore and aft in the plane of the ship's keel.

The fore-leech is nearly of the same depth as the fore-leech of the mizen-course, and the after-leech is from 2 to 4 yards deeper than the after-leech of the mizen-course.

GORES. The head, foot, and mast-leech are cut with a roach or curve; and as no strict rule can be laid down, the gores must be judiciously increased or diminished, according to the sweep required. The gore on the head is at the rate of from 9 to 12 inches per cloth; and on the foot, from 6 to 9 inches; or about 27 inches for every cloth in the mast-leech. From 4 to 6 cloths next the clue are cut square; or, the fifth cloth next the clue being square, the other four cloths are short-gored one inch per cloth to the clue. From four to six cloths are gored on the mast-leech; and if the depth of the leech be divided by the number of cloths in it, the quotient will be the regular gore per cloth, which must be augmented on the middle cloths, so as to form the sweep required.

The CLUE-LINING is two or three yards in length, and the TACK, NOCK, and PEEK PIECES are each one yard in length.

The SEAMS are 6 inches broad for 6 feet up the sail from the foot; and 2 inches broad for 4 feet down from the head: the remainder is one inch broad. The seams decrease gradually from one breadth to the other, but the selvage is not cut.

For TABLINGS and HEAD-HOLES consult the general instructions, pages 18—20.

Two inches of SLACK-CLOTH should be taken up with the rope in every yard in the mast-leech, and one inch in every cloth in the foot.

IRON THIMBLES are generally spliced in the rope at the tack, nock, and peek, which are otherwise fitted as the mizen-course.

The CLUE, likewise, is sometimes made with an iron thimble; but if not, it is made as described in the general instructions, page 25.

CRINGLES for the lacing are made on the mast-leech, 30 inches asunder.

To find the quantity of canvas, refer to Rule VII. page 35.

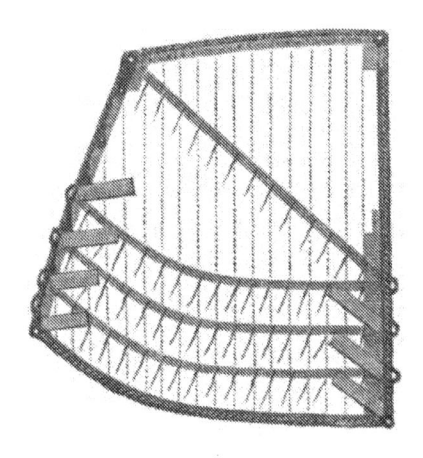

A BRIG'S MAIN-SAIL.

This sail is quadrilateral, and made of canvas No. 1 or 2. The fore-leech is in depth nearly the length of the main-mast from the under part of the hounds to the boom, and is fastened, in different places, to hoops which encircle the mast. The depth of the after-leech is about one-third more than the depth of the fore-leech. The head is bent to the gaff, and spreads within 9 inches of the cleats on the outer end; and the foot is extended by the boom, which hangs abaft the main-mast, and spreads within 18 inches of the sheave-hole at the outer end.

GORES. The head and mast-leech are sometimes gored with a small circular sweep, which must be regulated by practice. The *regular* gore on the head is from 4 to 5 inches per cloth, and the sweep may be cut after the sail is sewed together. The foot is gored with a circular sweep, at the rate of 5 or 7 inches per cloth, leaving 4 or 5 square cloths at the clue; or at the rate of 14 to 18 inches per cloth for every cloth in the mast-leech, which has 5 or 6 gored cloths in it.

The SEAMS are three inches broad for 8 feet up the sail from the foot, and two inches broad for 8 feet down from the head: the remainder is one inch broad; the seams decreasing gradually, as in the driver-boom-sail.

For TABLINGS and HEAD-HOLES, consult the general instructions, pages 18—20.

This sail has three REEF-BANDS, 6 inches broad, parallel to the foot. The upper one is nearly half-way up the fore-leech, and the others are at equal distances between that and the foot; it also sometimes has a BALANCE-REEF from the nock to the upper reef-cringle on the after-leech.

In the royal navy, main-sails have now STRENGTHENING-BANDS, running from the clue tack and each reef, in the manner delineated in the figure.

REEF-HANKS are generally sewed on the reef-bands: for the manner of doing which, see the general instructions, page 27.

LININGS. The after-leech is lined with one breadth of cloth from the clue to one yard above the upper reef-band; half a yard of the lining is cut down at the upper end, and the inner part is doubled under, or cut off. The PEEK-PIECE is one yard in length, and the fore-leech is lined with half a breadth of cloth; or sometimes pieces, one yard in length, are put on at the tack and nock, and small triangular pieces at each hole.

Four inches of SLACK-CLOTH should be taken up with the rope in every yard in the mast-leech.

Large IRON THIMBLES are stuck in the cringles at the clue, peek, nock, and tack; also in the cringles made on the leeches at the ends of the reef-bands; a luff-cringle is made on the mast-leech, equi-distant from the lower reef-band and the foot, which also has a thimble.

To find the quantity of canvas, refer to Rule VII. page 35.

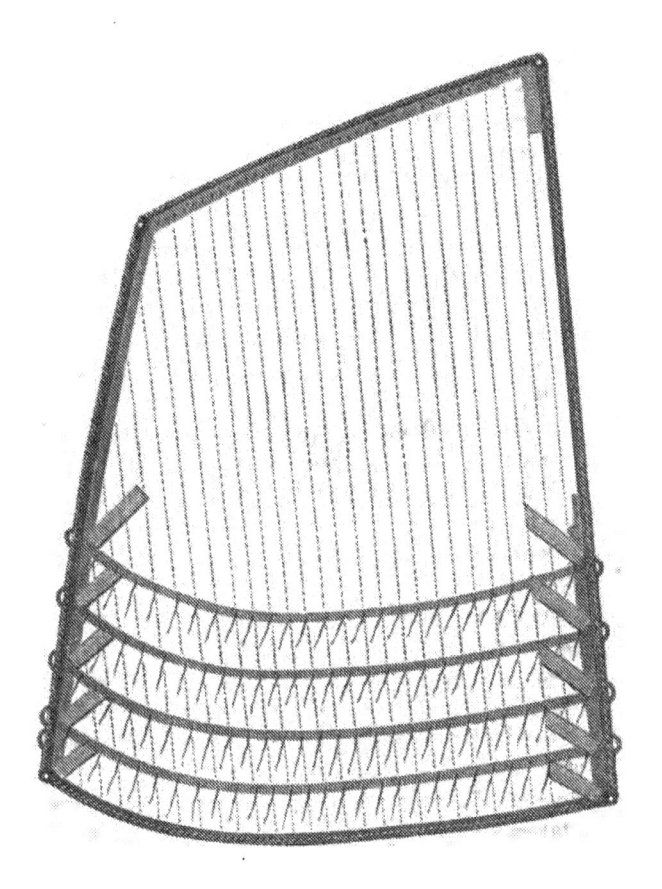

A CUTTER'S MAIN-SAIL.

This sail is quadrilateral, and made of canvas No. 1 or 2. The fore-leech is nearly of the depth of the mast from the under part of the hounds to the boom, and is fastened in different places to hoops which encircle the mast: the after-leech is about one-third deeper than the fore-leech. The head is bent to a gaff, and spreads within 18 inches of the cleats at the outer end; and the foot spreads within 2 or 3 feet of the sheave-hole at the outer end of the boom, which hangs fore and aft abaft the mast.

GORES. Six or eight cloths are gored on the fore-leech, and its length divided by the number of cloths gored gives the length of the gore on each cloth. The head is gored at the rate of 5 or 7 inches per cloth; and sometimes the fore-leech and head are cut with a small circular sweep, which must be cut by judgment, or after the sail is sewed together. The foot is gored with a circular sweep at the rate of 5 to 7 inches per cloth from the tack to the middle of the foot; then, two or three cloths being left square, the remaining cloths to the clue are gored at the rate of a full inch per cloth.

In the merchant-service, and for the custom, revenue, and smuggling, cutters, the head is generally wider, and peeks less, than in the royal navy. The former are better adapted for quick sailing, the latter for handsome appearance.

For TABLINGS and HEAD-HOLES, consult the general instructions, pages 18—20.

Four REEF-BANDS, 8 inches broad, are put on parallel to the foot; the upper one is about three-sevenths of the depth up the fore-leech from the foot, and the others at equal distances between that and the foot.

REEF-HANKS are generally sewed on the reef-bands, as on the brig's main-sail.

STRENGTHENING-BANDS, running from the clue tack and each reef, in the manner delineated in the figure.

The SEAMS are 5 inches broad for 12 feet up the sail from the foot, and 3 inches broad for 8 feet down from the head; the remainder is one inch and a half broad; the seams decreasing gradually from one breadth to another.

In sewing on the rope, four or five inches of SLACK-CLOTH should be taken up in every yard in the depth of the fore-leech.

Large IRON THIMBLES are stuck in the CRINGLES at the clue, peek, nock, and tack, and also in the REEF-CRINGLES, at the ends of the reef-bands. A LUFF-CRINGLE is made on the fore-leech between the lower reef-band and the tack, which also has a thimble.

To find the quantity of canvas, refer to Rule VII. page 35.

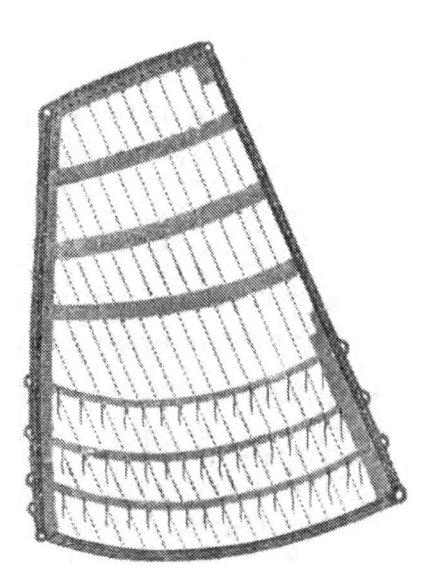

A CUTTER'S TRY-SAIL.

This sail is occasionally used, instead of the main-sail, in stormy weather, and is quadrilateral, generally cut square on the head, and made of canvas No. 1 or 2. It is extended as the main-sail, the fore-leech being attached to hoops which encircle the mast. The head is bent to a gaff, and the foot is extended by the boom or sheet to the horse.

In the head of the try-sail there are two-fifths of the number of cloths that are in the head of the main-sail: the fore-leech is about three-fourths of the depth of the fore-leech of the main-sail, and the after-leech is one-sixth deeper than the fore-leech.

GORES. Eight or ten cloths are gored on the fore-leech; and its depth, divided by the number of cloths, gives the length of each gore: if cut with a sweep, the gores can only be regulated by practice, or the sweep cut after the sail is sewed up. The foot is gored with a circular sweep at the rate of 5 or 7 inches per cloth from the tack, leaving 2 or 3 square cloths at the clue.

The SEAMS should be 5 inches broad for 12 feet up from the foot, and 3 inches broad for 8 feet down from the head; the remainder is one inch and a half broad. The seams decrease gradually from one breadth to another.

For TABLINGS and HEAD-HOLES, consult the general instructions, pages 18—20.

This sail has three REEF-BANDS, six inches wide, parallel with the foot; the upper one is three-eighths of the depth of the fore-leech from the foot, and the others are at equal distances between the foot and the upper one.

It also has three STRENGTHENING-BANDS of half a breadth of cloth, at equal distances between the upper reef-band and the head, which are seamed on, and stuck along the middle. These sails have frequently strengthening-bands, the same as the main-sail.

REEF-HANKS are generally sewed on the reef-bands, as on the brig's main-sail.

The after-leech is LINED with one breadth of cloth, from the clue to one yard and a half above the upper reef-band, where it is cut half-way across: and, one half of it being cut off, it is so continued about one yard higher.

Four or five inches of SLACK-CLOTH should be taken up with the rope in every yard in the fore-leech.

IRON THIMBLES are stuck in CRINGLES made at the clue, peek, nock, and tack; also in reef-cringles on the leeches at the ends of the reef-bands, and in a luff-cringle made on the fore-leech between the lower reef-cringle and the foot.

To find the quantity of canvas, refer to Rule VII. page 35.

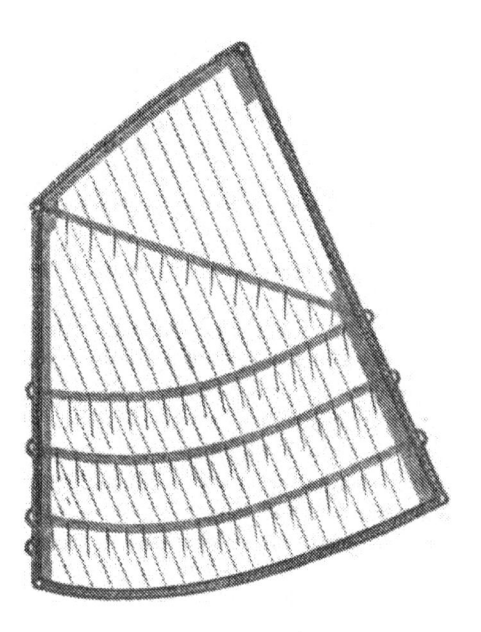

A SLOOP'S MAIN-SAIL.

This sail is quadrilateral, and made of canvas No. 1 or 2. The fore-leech is nearly of the depth of the mast from the under part of the hounds to the boom, and is attached to hoops which encircle the mast. The after-leech is about one-third deeper than the fore-leech. The head is bent to the gaff, and spreads within 12 inches of the outer end; and the foot is extended by the boom, which hangs fore-and-aft abaft the mast, and spreads within one or two feet of the sheave-hole at the outer end.

GORES. The head is gored at the rate of 3 to 6 inches per cloth, and is sometimes cut circular; and the foot is gored with a circular sweep, at the rate of 5 inches to $6\frac{1}{2}$ inches per cloth, 4 or 5 cloths next the clue being left square. The gore on the foot is governed by the number of cloths in the mast-leech: from 12 to 14 inches gore being allowed on each cloth in the foot, for every cloth in the mast-leech. From 6 to 8 cloths are gored on the fore-leech; and its depth, divided by that number of cloths, gives the length of each gore: it is sometimes cut circular.

For TABLINGS and HEAD-HOLES, consult the general instructions, pages 18—20.

This sail generally has three or four REEF-BANDS, 4 or 6 inches broad, parallel to the foot; the upper one is about half-way up the fore-leech, and the others are at equal distances between the upper one and the foot. Sometimes the reefs are fitted without bands. It also frequently has a balance-reef from the nock to the upper reef-cringle.

This sail has frequently STRENGTHENING-BANDS, the same as the brig's main-sail.

REEF-HANKS are generally sewed on the reef-bands, as on the brig's main-sail.

The after-leech is LINED with one breadth of cloth from the clue to two feet above the upper reef-band: this lining is cut down the middle at the upper end; and, half of it being cut away, the remaining part is so continued half a yard higher. The mast-leech is lined with half a breadth of cloth from the tack to the nock; and the PEEK-PIECE is one yard and a half in length. Sometimes pieces one yard and a quarter long are put on at the NOCK and TACK, and small triangular pieces at each hole instead of a mast-lining.

The SEAMS should be 4 inches broad for 9 feet up the seam from the foot: and 2 inches broad for 6 feet down the seam from the head; the remainder should be one full inch broad. The seams decrease gradually from one breadth to another.

The BOLT-ROPE on the mast-leech should be $2\frac{1}{2}$ or 3 inches in circumference; and on the head, foot, and after-leech, one inch and a half. Sometimes the foot-rope is not put on till the sail is half-worn.

When sewing on the rope, 4 inches of SLACK-CLOTH should be taken up in every yard in the mast-leech.

IRON THIMBLES are stuck in cringles at the tack, nock, peek, and clue. Thimbles are also stuck in cringles at the ends of the reef-bands, and in a luff-cringle on the mast-leech.

To find the quantity of canvas, refer to Rule VII. page 35.

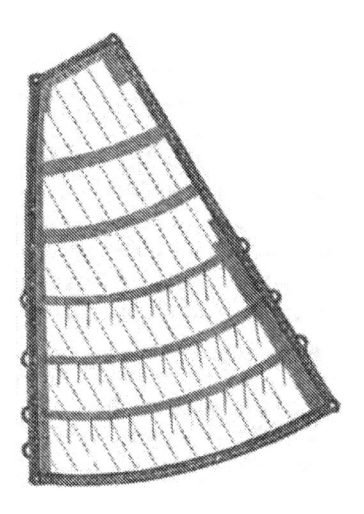

A SLOOP'S TRY-SAIL, OR STORM MAIN-SAIL.

This sail is quadrilateral, generally cut square on the head, and made of canvas No. 1 or 2. It is occasionally used for the main-sail in stormy weather. The fore-leech is from three-fourths of the depth to the same depth as the main-sail, and the after-leech is one-eighth deeper than the fore-leech. The head has two-fifths of the number of cloths that are in the head of the main-sail, and the foot is three times the breadth of the head.

This sail is extended as the main-sail; the fore-leech being attached to hoops which encircle the mast: the head is bent to a gaff, and the foot is extended by the boom or the stern.

GORES. Eight or ten cloths are gored on the fore-leech; and its depth, divided by the number of cloths, gives the length of each gore; if cut with a sweep, the gores can only be regulated by judgment. The foot is gored with a circular sweep, at the rate of 6 or 8 inches per cloth.

For TABLINGS and HEAD-HOLES, consult the general instructions, pages 18—20.

This sail has three or four REEF-BANDS, from 4 to 6 inches wide, parallel with the foot; the upper one is nearly half-way up the fore-leech, and the others are at equal distances between that and the foot. It also has two or three STRENGTHENING-BANDS, half a cloth broad, at equal distances asunder, above the upper reef-band, which are stuck or stitched along the middle. This sail has frequently strengthening-bands, the same as the brig's main-sail.

REEF-HANKS are generally sewed on the reef-bands, as on the brig's main-sail.

The AFTER-LEECH is lined with one breadth of cloth, from the clue to one yard and a quarter above the upper reef-band, which is there cut down the middle; and one part being cut away, the other is so continued about one yard higher. The fore-leech is lined with half a breadth of cloth, and the peek with a piece one yard and a half in length. Sometimes a piece, one yard in length, is put on at the nock.

The SEAMS should be 5 inches broad for 12 feet up the seam from the foot, and 3 inches broad for 8 feet down the seam from the head: the remainder is one inch and a half broad. The seams decrease gradually from one breadth to another.

The BOLT-ROPE for the mast-leech should be two inches and a half or three inches in circumference; for the head, foot, and after-leech, one inch and a half.

When sewing on the rope, 4 or 5 inches of SLACK-CLOTH should be taken up in every yard in the fore-leech.

IRON THIMBLES are stuck in the clue, peek, nock, and tack; also in the cringles at the ends of the reef-bands; and in a luff-cringle, made on the fore-leech, between the lower reef-cringle and the tack.

To find the quantity of canvas, refer to Rule VII. page 35.

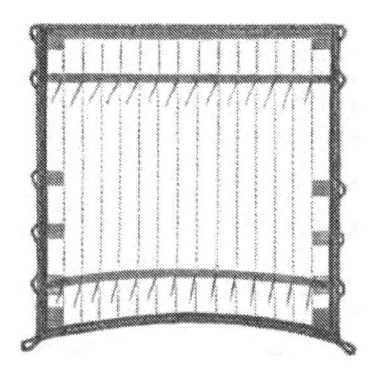

A SLOOP'S SQUARE-SAIL, OR CROSS-JACK.

This sail is quadrilateral, square on the head and leeches, and made of canvas No. 6 or 7. The head is bent to the cross-jack-yard, and it hangs at right angles with the ship's length, and parallel to the deck, extending within 6 inches of the cleats on the yard-arms. The depth of this sail is four-fifths of the depth of the fore-leech of the main-sail.

GORES. The foot is gored one inch per cloth, increasing to each clue: two or three square cloths being left in the middle.

For SEAMS, TABLINGS, and HEAD-HOLES, consult the general instructions, pages 17—20.

This sail has two REEF-BANDS, four inches broad; the lower one is at one-sixth of the depth of the sail from, and parallel to, the foot; and the upper one is at the same distance from the head.

REEF-HANKS are generally sewed on the reef-bands, as on the brig's main-sail.

LININGS. One yard of cloth is put on at each clue, half a yard at each earing, and half a yard against every cringle on the leeches. These linings are all put on the aft-side.

A REEF-CRINGLE is made at each end of the upper reef-band; and three bowline-cringles are made on each leech; the upper bowline-cringle is on the middle of the leech, and the others are equally distant from that and the clue.

Sometimes the clues are marled on; and, for this purpose, ten marling-holes are made each way from the clues; but consult the general instructions, page 24.

The BOLT-ROPE, on the foot and leeches, should be one inch and a half or two inches in circumference; and, on the head, one inch, or one inch and a half.

When sewing on the bolt-rope, one inch of SLACK-CLOTH should be taken up in every cloth in the head and foot.

To find the quantity of canvas, refer to Rule VI. page 34.

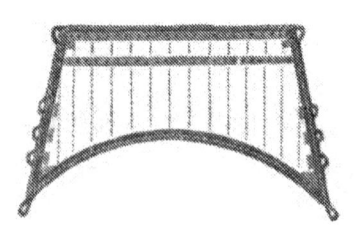

A SLOOP'S TOP-SAIL.

This sail is quadrilateal, square on the head, and made of canvas No. 6 or 7. It is bent at the head to the top-sail-yard, extending within 18 inches of the cleats, and hangs to the mast at right angles with the ship's length, and parallel to the cross-jack-yard. The depth in the middle is one-third of the depth of the cross-jack, or square-sail.

GORES. From one to two cloths are gored on the leeches, sufficiently for the foot to spread to the cleats on the cross-jack-yard; and the foot is hollowed from one-third to half of the depth of the sail in the middle (on account of the jib-stay), or at the rate of 10 or 12 inches per cloth from the middle to the clue, the middle cloth being left square.

For SEAMS, TABLINGS, REEF and HEAD HOLES, consult the general instructions, pages 17—20.

This sail has one REEF-BAND, four inches broad, at about one-third of the depth of the middle-cloth on the head.

LININGS. Pieces, half a yard in length, are put on at each earing; and six small pieces, cut out of half a yard of cloth, are put on the leeches, one against each bowline-cringle. The pieces are all put on the aft-side.

About three-quarters of an inch of SLACK-CLOTH should be taken up in every yard in the leeches, half an inch in every cloth in the head, and one inch in every cloth in the foot.

The BOLT-ROPE on the foot and leeches should be one inch and a half, or two inches, in circumference; and on the head one inch, or one inch and a half.

The CLUES are described in the general instructions, page 24.

Sometimes one REEF and three BOWLINE-CRINGLES are made on each leech. The reef-cringles are made at the ends of the reef-band; the upper bowline-cringle in the middle of the leech, and the others equally distant from that and the clue.

To find the quantity of canvas, refer to Rule I. page 30.

A SLOOP'S SAVE-ALL-TOP-SAIL.

This sail is quadrilateral, square on the head and foot, and made of canvas No. 8. The head is extended by haliards, fastened to its earing-cringles, in the upper part of the hollow foot of the top-sail, and the foot spreads the cross-jack-yard between the clues of the top-sail. It is seldom used but in calm weather.

GORES. Two or three cloths only are left square for the head, and the rest are gored for the leeches.

LININGS. The cloth at each clue is so cut as to fall to the foot, and form the clue-pieces.

The BOLT-ROPE on the head, foot, and leeches, should be one inch in circumference.

The CLUES are described in the general instructions, page 25.

To find the quantity of canvas, refer to Rule I. page 30.

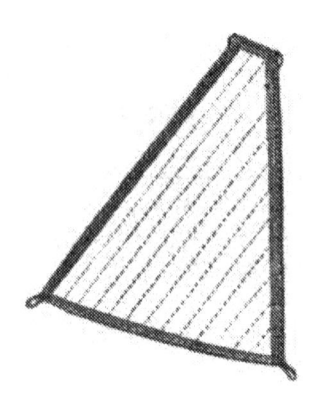

A SLOOP'S GAFF-TOP-SAIL.

This sail is quadrilateral, and sometimes triangular, and made of canvas No. 8. The fore-leech is four-fifths of the depth of the fore-leech of the main-sail, and is attached to the top-gallant-mast; the head is bent to a small gaff or yard, by which it is hoisted to the top-gallant-mast-head, and the foot spreads the gaff of the main-sail. This sail is only used in light breezes.

GORES. The depth of the gore on each cloth in the mast-leech is found by dividing the depth of the leech by the number of cloths. The head is gored 6 or 8 inches per cloth, and the foot 6 or 8 inches per cloth: a short gore to the clue, that the foot may answer the peek of the main-sail.

The BOLT-ROPE on the fore-leech should be one inch and a half in circumference; and on the head, foot, and after-leech, one inch.

The CLUE is described in the general instructions, page 25.

To find the quantity of canvas, refer to Rule IV. page 33.

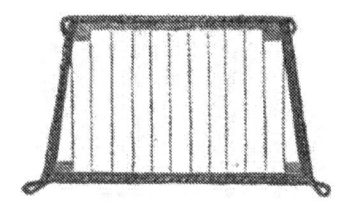

A SLOOP'S TOP-GALLANT-SAIL.

This sail is quadrilateral, cut square on the head and foot, and made of canvas No. 8. It is bent on the head to the top-gallant-yard, which hangs above the top-sail-yard at right angles with the vessel's length. The head spreads the top-gallant-yard, and extends within six inches of the cleats; and the foot spreads to the cleats on the top-sail-yard. This sail is from 3 to 5 yards deep, or the depth of the leeches of the top-sail.

GORES. One or more cloths are gored on the leeches.

LININGS. Sometimes pieces, half a yard in length, are put on the aft-side of the sail at the clues and earings.

For SEAMS, TABLINGS, and HEAD-HOLES, consult the general instructions, pages 17—20.

The BOLT-ROPE on the foot and leeches should be one inch in circumference; and on the head three-quarters of an inch, or one inch.

One inch of SLACK-CLOTH should be taken up with the rope in every cloth in the foot, and three-quarters of an inch in every yard in the leeches.

The CLUES are described in the general instructions, page 25.

To find the quantity of canvas, refer to Rule I. page 30.

A SLOOP'S WATER-SAIL.

This sail is quadrilateral, cut square on the head, and made of canvas No. 7. It is occasionally spread under the boom of the main-sail in fair wind. The depth of the sail is from one-half to three-fourths of the length of the boom, and it is 4 or 5 cloths wide.

GORES. The leeches are either cut square, or have one gored cloth.

For SEAMS, TABLINGS, and HEAD-HOLES, consult the general instructions, pages 17—20.

The BOLT-ROPE on the head, foot, and leeches should be one inch and a half in circumference.

The CLUES are described in the general instructions, page 25.

To find the quantity of canvas, refer to Rule VI. page 34.

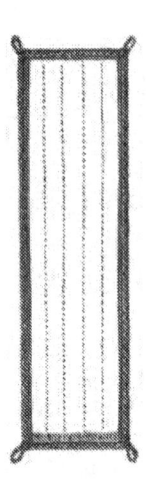

When sloops have lower-studding-sails, they are similar to the water-sail; the leeches are square, and they are one yard deeper than the leech of the cross-jack, or square-sail.

Some ships have a water-sail, similar to a sloop's water-sail.

A SLOOP'S FORE-SAIL.

This sail is triangular, made of canvas No. 1 or 2, and bends with hanks to the stay next before the mast. The depth of the leech is nearly the same as the depth of the foremost leech of the main-sail; and there are as many cloths in the foot as will bring it clear of the mast.

GORES. The depth of the hoist, or fore-part, divided by the number of gored cloths, gives the length of each gore. The foot has a short gore, of one inch per cloth, increasing to the clue; leaving one or two square cloths at the tack.

The leech-cloth is left three-quarters of a yard longer than the depth of the leech, for the HEAD-LINING and TABLING; and the cloth at the tack is so cut as to fall to the foot, and form its own LINING.

The SEAMS should be three or four inches wide at the foot, and decreasing to one inch at the hoist.

Two REEF-BANDS, 4 inches broad, are generally put on at one-eighth of the depth of the sail asunder; the lower one being at that distance from the foot. Sometimes a bonnet is used instead of the lower reef.

REEF-HANKS are generally sewed on, instead of using reef-points; for which see page 27.

The leech is LINED with a breadth of cloth from the clue to half a yard above the upper reef-band, where it is cut half-way across:

and, one-half of it being cut away, the other part is so continued about one yard higher. Sometimes small triangular pieces are sewed on at each hole in the hoist.

The BOLT-ROPE on the stay should be 2½ or 3 inches in circumference, and on the foot and leech 1½ or 2 inches.

Three or four inches of SLACK-CLOTH should be taken up with the rope in every yard in the hoist.

The HOIST-ROPE is put through the holes in the head-stick; then served with spunyarn, and spliced into the leech-rope. The middle of the head-stick is then seized to the head of the sail; and a thimble is seized in the bight of the rope.

THIMBLES are generally stuck in the cringles at the tack and clue, as mentioned in page 25.

To find the quantity of canvas, refer to Rule VIII. page 36.

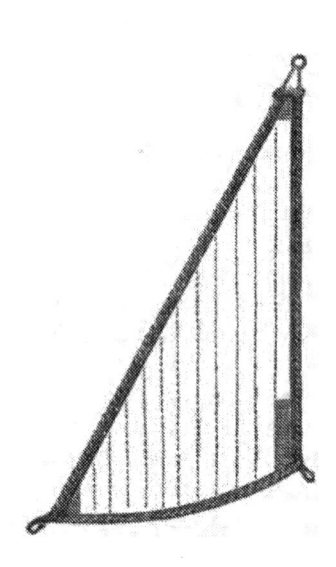

A SLOOP'S JIB.

This sail is triangular, made of canvas No. 2 to 6, and is sometimes bent to hanks on the stay before the fore-sail. The depth of the leech is one yard for every cloth in the foot, and the foot is made wide enough to spread the bowsprit.

GORES. The depth of the hoist, or fore-part, divided by the number of cloths gored, gives the length of each gore. The foot is gored with a sweep, at the rate of 5 or 6 inches per cloth, increasing to the clue; leaving one square cloth at the tack.

The leech-cloth is left three-quarters of a yard longer than the depth of the leech, for the HEAD-LINING and TABLING; the cloth at the TACK is so cut as to fall to the foot and form its own lining; and the CLUE-PIECE is two yards in length.

The SEAMS on the foot should be 3 or 4 inches broad, and should decrease to one full inch on the hoist.

BOLT-ROPE. If hoisted with a stay, the rope on the hoist should be 2½ or 3 inches in circumference; but if not hoisted with a stay, the rope on the hoist should be five inches. The rope on the foot and leeches should be two inches and a half.

Four or five inches of SLACK-CLOTH should be taken up in every yard in the hoist, when sewing on the rope, and the rope on the hoist put through the holes in the head-stick; then served with spunyarn, and spliced into the leech-rope.

The HEAD-STICK is seized round the middle to the head of the sail, and a thimble seized in the bight of the rope.

THIMBLES are generally stuck in the cringles at the tack and clue. This sail sometimes has a bonnet.

To find the quantity of canvas, refer to Rule VIII. page 36.

Observe, that the sloop's second jib is seven-eighths of the size of the first jib; the third jib is three-fourths of the size of the first jib; but they are both made like the first jib, as above.

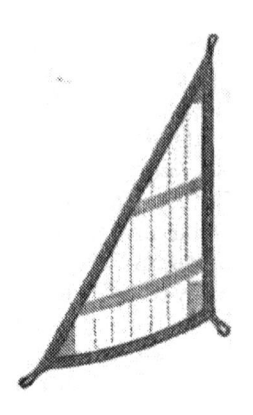

A SLOOP'S STORM-JIB.

This sail is triangular, and made of canvas No. 1 or 2. It is two-thirds of the size of the first jib, and is used in stormy weather, in lieu of a larger one.

Gores. The depth of the hoist, divided by the number of gored cloths in it, gives the length of each gore. The foot is gored at the rate of 5 or 6 inches per cloth, increasing to the clue.

The seams should be 3 or 4 inches broad at the foot, and should decrease to one inch on the hoist. The bolt-rope on the hoist should be five inches in circumference, and on the foot and leech two inches and a half.

Two strengthening-bands of half a breadth of cloth are put on parallel to the foot, at one-third of the depth of the sail asunder.

The clue is lined with a breadth of cloth one yard and a half in length; a piece, one yard long, is put on at the peek; and the cloth at the tack is so cut as to fall to the foot, and form its own lining.

Thimbles are sometimes seized in the peek, tack, and clue.

To find the quantity of canvas, refer to Rule VIII. page 36.

A SLOOP'S FLYING-JIB.

This sail is triangular, made of canvas No. 6, and is two-thirds of the size of the first jib. It is the foremost sail, and hoists without a stay.

GORES. The depth of the hoist, or fore-part, divided by the number of cloths, gives the length of each gore. The foot is gored with a sweep, at the rate of 8 or 9 inches per cloth, increasing to the clue.

The PIECE at the CLUE is one yard and a half in length; that at the PEEK is one yard; and the cloth at the TACK is so cut as to fall to the foot, and form its own LINING.

The SEAMS should be two inches and a half broad at the foot, and should decrease to one inch at the hoist.

The ROPE on the hoist should be three inches and a half in circumference; on the foot, two inches; and, on the leech, one inch.

Three inches of SLACK-CLOTH should be taken up with the rope in every yard in the hoist.

THIMBLES are sometimes spliced in the tack and peek.

The CLUE is described in the general instructions, page 25.

To find the quantity of canvas, refer to Rule VIII. page 36.

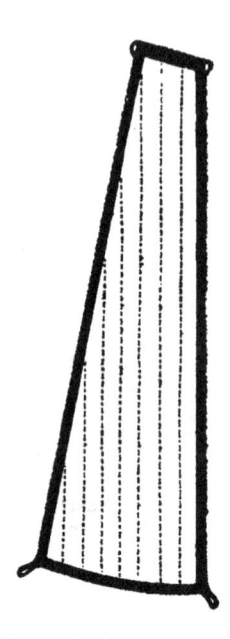

A SLOOP'S RINGTAIL-SAIL.

This sail is quadrilateral, and made of canvas No. 7 or 8. It is occasionally hoisted abaft the after-leech of the main-sail, to which the fore-leech is made to answer. The head is bent to a small yard at the outer end of the gaff; and the foot is spread on the boom, which is prolonged by a piece lashed to the outer end.

GORES. The depth of the fore-leech, being divided by the number of cloths in it, gives the length of the gore on each cloth. The head has a regular gore to answer the peek of the main-sail, and the foot is gored with a gore of one inch per cloth, increasing to the tack.

The BOLT-ROPE on the head, foot, and after-leech, should be one inch in circumference; and, on the fore-leech, one inch and a half.

A sail of this kind, but more square, is sometimes extended in light winds, on a small mast, erected for that purpose on the upper part of the stern of some vessels; the foot being spread out by a boom that projects horizontally from the stern.

The CLUES are described in the general instructions, page 25.

To find the quantity of canvas, refer to Rule IV. page 33.

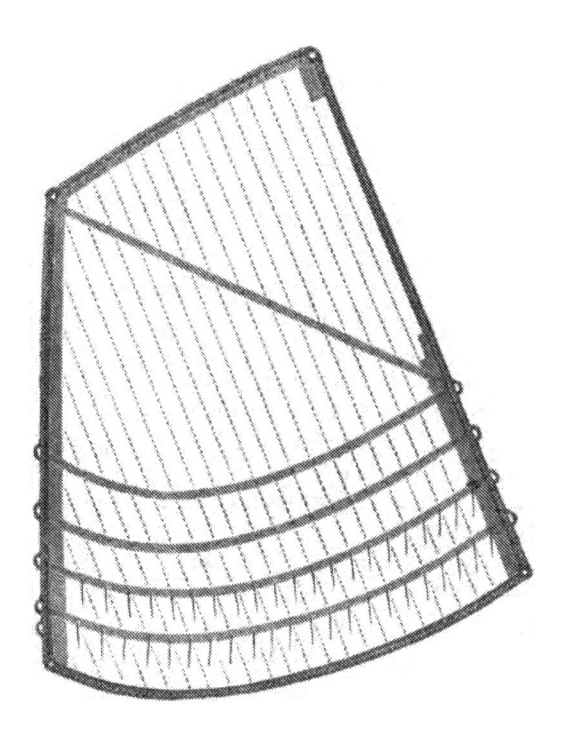

A SMACK'S MAIN-SAIL.

This sail is quadrilateral, and made of canvas No. 1 or 2. The fore-leech is nearly of the depth of the mast from the under part of the hounds to the boom, and is attached to hoops which encircle the mast. The after-leech is about one-fifth deeper than the fore-leech. The head is bent to the gaff, and spreads within 12 inches of the cleats at the outer end; and the foot is spread upon the boom, extending within 18 inches of the sheave-hole at the outer end of it.

GORES. The depth of the fore-leech, divided by the number of cloths to the mast, gives the length of the regular gore per cloth; but, if cut with a sweep, the gores must be regulated by judgment. The head is gored at the rate of 4 or 5 inches per cloth; and the foot, with a circular sweep, at the rate of 12 or 14 inches per cloth, for every cloth in the mast-leech, it having a short gore to the clue on 5 or 6 cloths, at the rate of 3 or 4 inches per cloth.

The FORE-LEECH is LINED with a breadth of cloth, from the tack to the nock; and the AFTER-LEECH is lined with a breadth of cloth from the clue to two yards above the upper reef-band, where it is cut half way across: and, one part being cut away, the other is so continued about one yard higher. The PEEK is lined with a piece one yard and a half in length.

The SEAMS should be 4 inches broad 9 feet up from the foot, and 2 inches broad 6 feet down from the head; the remainder of the seam should be one inch broad.

Four REEF-BANDS, from 6 to 8 inches broad, are put on parallel with the foot: the upper one is at three-sevenths of the depth of the fore-leech from the foot, and the others are at equal distances from the upper one. Sometimes a BALANCE-REEF is put on from the nock to the upper reef-cringle on the after-leech.

REEF-HANKS are generally sewed on, instead of using reef-points; for which see page 28.

For TABLINGS and HEAD-HOLES, consult the general instructions, pages 18—27.

The BOLT-ROPE on the mast-leech should be three inches in circumference, and, on the head, foot, and after-leech, one inch and a half.

Four inches of SLACK-CLOTH should be taken up with the rope in every yard in the mast-leech.

IRON THIMBLES are stuck in the CRINGLES at the tack, nock, peek, and clue; in cringles made on each leech, at the ends of the reef-bands, and in a luff-cringle made on the fore-leech between the lower reef-cringle and the tack.

To find the quantity of canvas, refer to Rule VII. page 35.

A SMACK'S FORE-SAIL.

This sail is triangular, made of canvas No. 1 or 2, and bends with hanks to the stay next before the mast. The leech is of the same depth as the fore-leech of the main-sail, and there are as many cloths in the foot as will keep clear of the mast.

GORES. The depth of the hoist, divided by the number of cloths, gives the length of the gore on each cloth. The foot is gored with a short gore, increasing to the clue, of one inch per cloth, leaving two or three square cloths at the tack.

The LEECH-CLOTH is cut square at the upper end, and is so doubled as to form its own LINING. The cloth at the TACK is cut in the same manner. The LEECH is LINED with a breadth of cloth from the clue to one yard and a half above the upper reef-band, where it is cut half across; and one part being cut away, the other part is so continued about one yard higher.

A broad TABLING is generally made on the hoist, but sometimes small triangular pieces are put on at each hole instead of it.

STAY-HOLES are made, one on each seam.

The SEAMS should be 3 or 4 inches wide at the foot, and to decrease to one full inch at the hoist.

Two REEF-BANDS, four inches broad, are sometimes put on parallel to the foot, at about one-ninth of the depth of the leech asunder; but a bonnet is more frequently used to this sail.

REEF-HANKS are generally sewed on, instead of using reef-points, for which see page 27.

The BOLT-ROPE on the stay should be two inches and a half, or three inches, in circumference; and on the foot and leech, one inch and a half or two inches.

Three or four inches of SLACK-CLOTH should be taken up with the rope in every yard in the hoist.

IRON THIMBLES are generally stuck in the cringles at the tack and clue, and in the bight of the rope at the peek. Sometimes this sail has a head-stick.

To find the quantity of canvas, refer to Rule VIII. page 36.

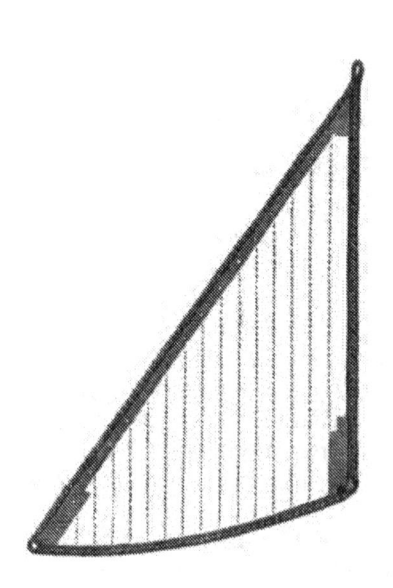

A SMACK'S JIB.

This sail is triangular, made of canvas No. 1 or 2, and generally hoists by haliards, without a stay, next before the fore-sail. The foot is made to spread the bowsprit, and the depth of the leech is from three-quarters of a yard to one yard for every cloth in the foot.

GORES. The depth of the hoist, or fore-part, divided by the number of cloths, gives the length of each gore. The fourth and fifth cloths from the tack are cut square on the foot, and the cloths each way from them are gored with a sweep, at one inch per cloth, increasing to the tack and clue.

The upper end of the LEECH-CLOTH is cut square, and is doubled back to form its own LINING. The TACK and CLUE are LINED with a breadth of cloth two yards in length. When this sail is made to hoist with a stay, it either has small triangular pieces put on at each hole in the hoist, or a broad tabling.

STAY-HOLES are made, one on each seam.

The SEAMS should be 3 or 4 inches wide at the foot, and to decrease to one full inch at the hoist.

The ROPE on the stay should be five inches in circumference; and that on the foot and leech two inches.

Four or five inches of SLACK-CLOTH should be taken up with the rope in every yard in the hoist.

THIMBLES are stuck in the cringles at the tack and clue; and one is seized in the bight of the rope at the peek, which is seized with spunyarn.

This sail sometimes has a HEAD-STICK.

To find the quantity of canvas, refer to Rule VIII. page 36.

SKY-SCRAPERS.

These sails are triangular, and made of canvas No. 8. The foot spreads half of the royal-yards, and each sail has half the number of cloths in the foot as are in the head of its respective royal-sail. The peek is hoisted by a haliard to the truck on the mast-head.

To find the quantity of canvas, refer to Rule III. page 32.

This sail is very seldom used, and is not usually made in the general practice.

THE UNDERMENTIONED SAILS ARE VERY SELDOM USED; AND ARE NOT USUALLY MADE IN THE GENERAL PRACTICE.

ROYAL STAY-SAILS are quadrilateral, and made of canvas No. 8. They are the same as a top-gallant-stay-sail, only with one or two cloths less, and are hoisted next above them.

To find the quantity of canvas, refer to Rule V. page 34.

STORM-MIZEN. This sail is triangular, and similar to a fore-top-mast-stay-sail. It is made of canvas No. 2 or 3, and bends on the fore part to a horse, abaft and parallel to the mizen-mast. The foot is extended towards the tafferel by a sheet.

To find the quantity of canvas, refer to Rule III. page 32.

SPRIT-SAIL-TOP-GALLANT-SAIL is quadrilateral, cut square on the head, and is similar to the sprit-sail-top-sail. It is made of canvas No. 8, and is bent on the head to the sprit-sail-top-gallant-sail-yard, which hangs at right angles under the outer end of the jib-boom. The foot spreads the sprit-sail-top-sail-yard, and contains the same number of cloths in it as the head of the sprit-sail-top-sail. One or two cloths are gored on each leech.

To find the quantity of canvas, refer to Rule I. page 30.

WING-SAIL FOR KETCHES. This sail is quadrilateral, and similar to the mizen-course of a ship. It is made of canvas No. 6 or 7, and bends abaft the main-mast to hoops which encircle the mast. The head is extended by a gaff.

To find the quantity of canvas, refer to Rule II. page 31.

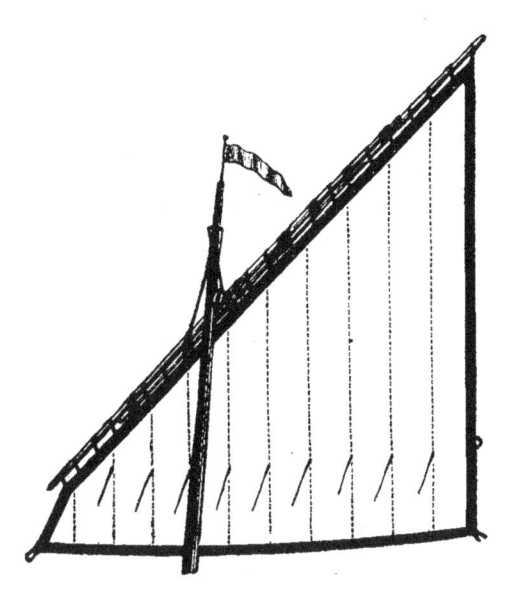

A BOAT'S SETTEE-SAIL.

This sail is quadrilateral, and made of canvas No. 7 or 8. The head is bent to a lateen-yard, which hangs obliquely to the mast, at one-third of its length, and extends within six inches of the cleats.

GORES. The cloth at the tack is cut goring to the nock, and the bunt is of the depth of the reef, which is one-fifth the depth of the leech. The leech is five-sixths of the length of the head. The length of the head, divided by the number of cloths in it, gives the length of each gore. The foot is cut with a circular sweep, after the sail is sewed together.

Two small HOLES are made in each cloth, along the head; and holes are made across the sail, on each seam, at one-fifth of the depth of the leech from the foot, for the REEF.

REEF-HANKS are used instead of reef-points; for which see page 27.

A small REEF-CRINGLE is made on the after-leech-rope, and CRINGLES are made at the nock and peek.

To find the quantity of canvas, refer to Rule IV. page 33.

A BOAT'S LATTEEN-SAIL.

This sail is triangular, and made of canvas No. 7 or 8. It is so called from its head being bent to the latteen-yard, which hangs obliquely to the mast at one-third of its length, extending within six inches of the cleats.

Gores. The length of the head, divided by the number of cloths, gives the length of the gore on each cloth. The foot is cut square.

Two small holes are made in each cloth along the head, through which the lacings are reeved.

To find the quantity of canvas, refer to Rule III. page 32.

A BOAT'S SLIDING-GUNTER-SAIL.

This sail is the same as the boat's latteen-sail; but it is thus called when the head of it (then called the fore-leech) is laced to a mast and top-mast, the top-mast being made to slide down the mast by means of hoops.

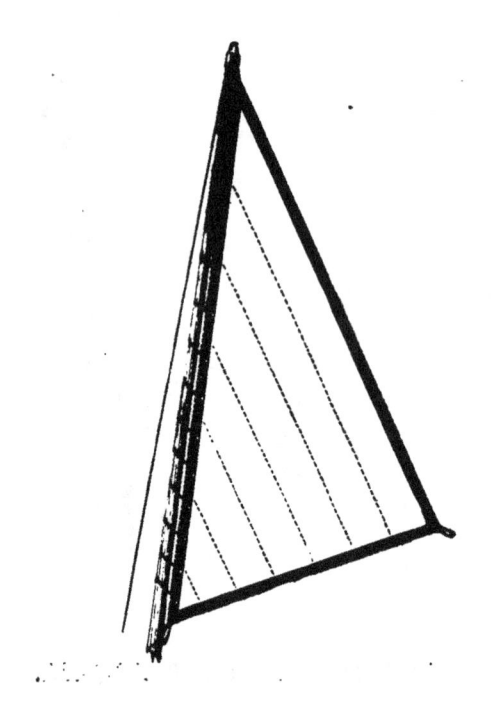

A BOAT'S SHOULDER-OF-MUTTON-SAIL.

This is the same as the boat's lateen-sail, but is called a SHOULDER-OF-MUTTON-SAIL, when laced by the fore-leech to a single mast.

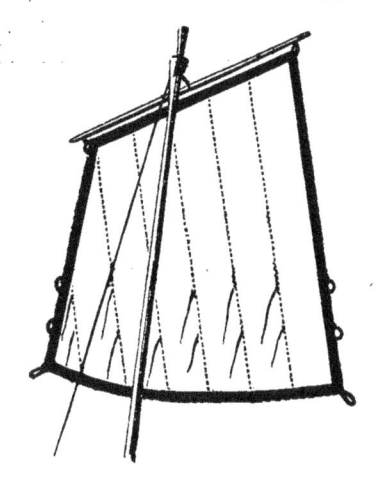

A BOAT'S LUG-SAIL.

This sail is quadrilateral, and made of canvas No. 7 or 8. The head is bent to a yard, which hangs obliquely to the mast at one-third of its length, and extends within 4 inches of the cleats.

The fore-leech is as deep as the length of the head, and the after-leech is longer than the fore-leech by nearly half the depth of the fore-leech.

GORES. Two or three cloths are gored on the fore-leech, and an even gore of 6 inches per cloth is made on the head. The foot is gored with a sweep; the cloth at the clue being cut with a three-inch short gore, the next cloth is square, and the cloths from thence to the tack are gored at the rate of six or eight inches per cloth.

Two small HOLES are made in each cloth in the head.

This sail has two REEFS parallel with the foot; the upper one is half-way up the fore-leech, and the other is equally distant from that and the foot. Sometimes REEF-BANDS, three or four inches broad, are put on at the reefs, but when these are not used, a small hole is made in every seam instead of them.

REEF-MANKS are used instead of reef-points; for which see page 27.

110   THE PRACTICE OF SAIL-MAKING.

Small CRINGLES are made on the leeches at each reef; EARING-CRINGLES are made at the nock and peek; and 10 or 12 strands in the length of the rope are seized at the TACK and CLUE.

To find the quantity of canvas, refer to Rule IX. page 37.

A BOAT'S MAIN-SPRIT-SAIL.

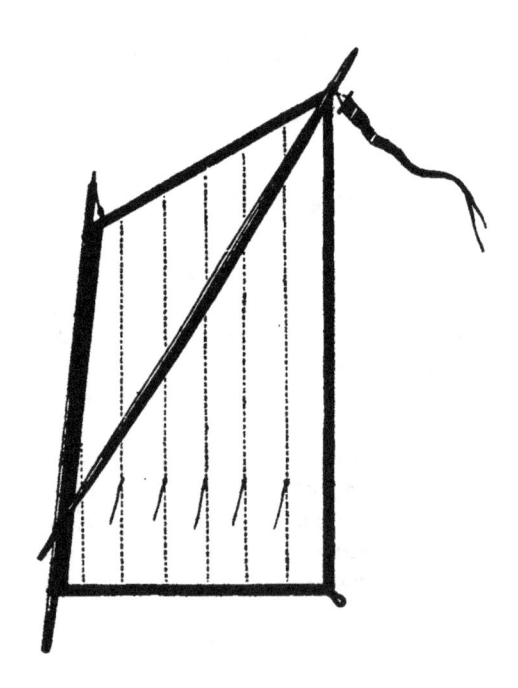

BOATS' SPRIT-SAILS.

These sails are quadrilateral, and made of canvas No. 7 or 8: the fore-leeches are attached to their respective masts by lacings, reeved through holes made in them; and the heads are elevated

A BOAT'S FORE-SPRIT-SAIL.

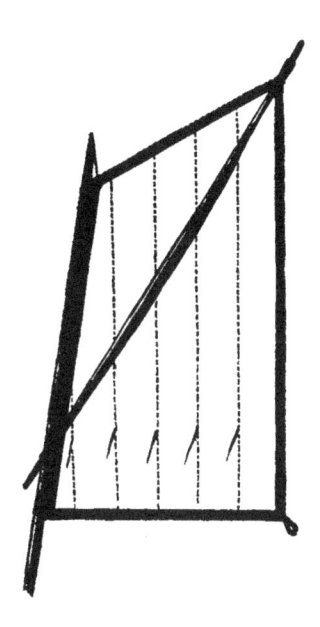

BOATS' SPRIT-SAILS, CONTINUED.

and extended by sprits, or small yards, that cross the sail diagonally from the mast to the peek; the lower end of the sprit rests in a wreath or collar of rope called a snotter, which encircles the mast at the foot of the sail.

GORES. The fore-leeches of the MAIN and FORE SPRIT-SAILS are the depth of the mast within twelve inches of the gunwale, and have one or two gored cloths. The heads of them have an even gore of 12 or 14 inches per cloth.

The fore-leech of the MIZEN-SPRIT-SAIL is the depth of the

A BOAT'S MIZEN-SPRIT-SAIL.

BOATS' SPRIT-SAILS, CONTINUED.

mast, so as to clear the gunwale, and is square. The head has an even gore of 11 inches per cloth.

Small HOLES are made in the fore-leeches: those in the main and fore sprit-sails are one in each yard, and those in the mizen are three-quarters of a yard asunder. Holes are also made in the seams, across the sail, at one-fifth of the depth of the after-leech from the foot, for the reef.

REEF-HANKS are used instead of reef-points; for which see page 27.

Ten or twelve turns or twists of the strands in the length of the rope is seized, to form bights, at the TACK, NOCK, PEEK, and CLUE.

To find the quantity of canvas, refer to Rule IV. page 33.

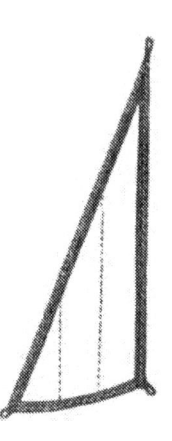

A BOAT'S FORE-SAIL.

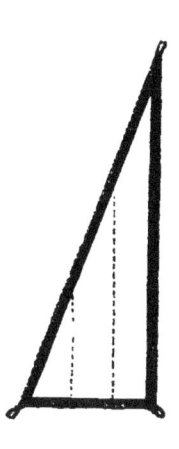

This sail is triangular, and made of canvas No. 8. The leech is of the same depth as the fore-leech of the fore-sprit-sail, and the foot is made wide enough to spread from the stem to the mast.

GORES. The depth of the fore-part, or hoist, divided by the number of cloths, gives the length of each gore. The foot is cut square.

Two inches of SLACK-CLOTH should be taken up with the rope in every yard in the depth of the hoist.

To find the quantity of canvas, refer to Rule III. page 32.

A BOAT'S JIB.

This sail is triangular, and made of canvas No. 8. The leech is of the same depth as the leech of the fore-sail, and the foot is as wide as the length of the bowsprit.

GORES. The depth of the fore-part, or hoist, divided by the number of cloths, gives the length of each gore. The foot is cut with a sweep, at the rate of 6 or 7 inches per cloth, with a short gore to the clue.

Two inches of SLACK-CLOTH should be taken up with the rope in every yard in the hoist.

To find the quantity of canvas, refer to Rule VIII. page 36.

MAST-COATS.

Mast-coats are made of canvas No. 1 or 2, to fit round the mast and hole in the deck. When fixed, they have the shape of a cone.

Girth the mast about, at 18 inches above the deck, and girth round the deck, at three inches from the mast-hole: this gives the circumference at top and bottom. The length is obtained by measuring strait the distance between the places girthed.

Divide the lower girths into an equal number of parts, suitably to the width of the canvas, allowing for the SEAMS, which are one inch wide. The cloths must be gored upwards, to produce the circumference of the mast at the top-girth, and when sewed together, cut with a sweep, to set neatly round the mast. The upper part is then sewed into a double canvas collar, six inches wide.

To find the quantity of canvas in mast-coats, multiply the number of cloths by the length, and add the quantity in the collar.

EXAMPLE.

	Ft.	In.	
	1	8	Length
		4	Number of cloths
	6	8	
	3		Feet in the collar
Total	9	8	or 3¼ Yards.

RUDDER-COATS.

RUDDER-COATS are made of canvas No. 1 or 2, to fit round the rudder and the hole in the counter. Girth the circumference of the rudder-hole; then round the rudder and part of the stern-post about four feet below the counter. This gives the width at top and bottom. The length is obtained by measuring the distance between the places girthed.

Divide the upper girths into an equal number of breadths, suitably to the canvas, allowing for the seams. The cloths are GORED downwards with a small sweep, that the coat may bag, and not set too tight when fixed. The SEAMS are one inch wide, and a two or three inch tabling is made all round.

To find the quantity of canvas in a rudder-coat, multiply the number of cloths by the length of the coat.

EXAMPLE.

	Ft.	In.	
	4	9	Length of the coat.
		6	Number of cloths.
Total	28	6	or 9½ Yards.

WIND-SAIL, OR VENTILATOR.

The wind-sail or ventilator is made of canvas No. 1 or 2. It is used for circulating fresh air between deck, and is in the form of a cylinder.

Four breadths are sewed together, and the outer selvages joined, with an inch SEAM, leaving one cloth four feet short of the top.

A three inch TABLING goes round the top and bottom. It is kept distended by CIRCULAR HOOPS, made of ash, sewed to the inside; one at top, and one at every six feet distance. The upper part, or top, is covered with canvas, and a small rope sewed round the edge; into which are spliced, at the quarters, the ends of two pieces of rope, that are sewed up to the middle, and an eye formed by seizing the bights. The length of a wind-sail is taken nine feet above the deck to three or four feet below the lower hatchway.

To find the quantity of canvas in the ventilator, multiply the number of cloths by the length.

EXAMPLE.

4 Number of cloths.
9 Yards in length.

Total 36 Yards.

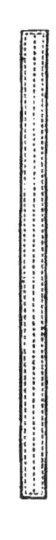

QUARTER-CLOTHS.

Quarter-cloths are made of canvas No. 1 or 2. They are extended from the rough-tree-rail of the quarter-deck to the plank-sheer.

The LENGTH is taken from the aft part of the stern, along the rough-tree-rail upon the quarter, to the haunch, or where the rail ends.

The DEPTHS are taken from the rail to the plank-sheer, at the fore part of the rail, at the taffarel, and at the midway between. They contain in general two whole cloths, and one gored cloth, which is always placed at the lower part.

The SEAMS are one inch broad, and a two or three inch TABLING is made all round.

To find the quantity of canvas in quarter-cloths, multiply the number of whole cloths by the length, and add the quantity in the gored cloth.

To find the quantity in the gored cloth, take the breadth of the gored cloth at the ends and in the middle; add them together, and divide their sum by three for a medium breadth. Then multiply that medium breadth by the length of the cloth.

EXAMPLE.

```
        20  Yards, length.
         2  Number of whole cloths.
        ——
        40  Yards.
        6¾  ······ in the gored cloth.
        ——
Total   46¾ Yards in the quarter-cloth.
```

To find the quantity in the gored cloth.

```
Breadth at the fore part of the rail  12 Inches.
·············· middle ············     8
············ aft-part ··········       4
                                      ——
                                   3)24
                                      ——
                                       8 inches, or ⅓ of a breadth multiplied
                                         by 20 yards, the length is 6 yards,
                                         24 inches.
```

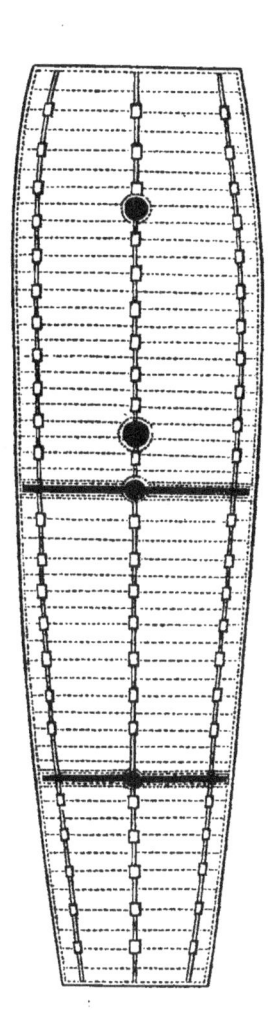

AWNINGS.

Awnings are made of canvas No. 1 or 2.

The LENGTH of the MAIN-DECK AWNING is from the centre of the fore-mast to the centre of the main-mast. The WIDTH is shaped agreeably to the breadths of the ship, taken at the main-mast, the fore-mast, and at the midway between.

The LENGTH of the QUARTER-DECK-AWNING is from the centre of the main-mast to the centre of the mizen-mast. The WIDTH is shaped agreeably to the breadths of the ship, taken at the main-mast, the mizen-mast, and at the midway between.

The LENGTH of the POOP or AFTER-AWNING is from the centre of the mizen-mast to the ensign-staff, about seven feet above the deck. The width is shaped agreeably to the breadths of the ship, taken at the mizen-mast, the taffarel, and at the midway between.

Vessels in harbour, particularly in the royal navy, have uprights (instead of masts), one fixed at the break of the quarter-deck, one at the forecastle, and one at the knight-heads forward. The lengths and breadths are taken as before, only at those uprights instead of at the masts.

The canvas is cut out to the given breadths of the awning, allowing about nine inches to hang down on each side, which is sometimes scolloped and bound with green baize, and is sewed together with an inch SEAM, and TABLED all round with a two or three inch tabling. Half the diameter of the masts is cut out in the middle at each end, and LACING-HOLES are made across the ends to connect one awning to another.

On the upper part, along the middle and sides, is sewed one inch and half or two inch rope, to which the TRUCKS are sewed at about three-quarters of a yard asunder. A THIMBLE is spliced in each end of the rope.

Sometimes CURTAINS are made to hang to the sides of the awnings, of the same length as the awnings. Their depth is taken from the sides of the awning to the gunwale, supposing the awning to be in its place. The SEAMS and TABLINGS are the same as those of the awnings, and LACING-HOLES are made along the upper tabling of the curtain, and the side tabling of the awning.

To find the quantity of canvas in awnings, multiply the number of cloths by the medium breadth. The medium breadth is found by adding together the three breadths, and dividing the sum by three.

To find the quantity in the curtain, multiply the number of cloths by the length.

Example of a MAIN-DECK AWNING.

```
Breadth at main-mast·  9
··········  fore-mast··  8
··········  midway  ···10
           ─────
           3)27      24  Number of cloths.
           ─────      9  Yards, medium breadth.
           Total 216
```

Example for the CURTAIN.

```
 4  Number of cloths.
15  Yards in length.
───
60  Yards.
```

A SMOKE-SAIL.

This sail is quadrilateral, square on the head and foot, and made of canvas No. 1 or 2. It is extended to a small yard by the earings at the head, and by sheets at the foot, near the aft part of the forecastle, to prevent the smoke from the galley-chimney coming aft.

The leeches are commonly square, or may be gored half a cloth, as has been recommended.

The number of the cloths is about one-fourth of the cloths in the fore-course. The depth is one-half of the depth of the fore-course.

The roping and rule to find the contents as the top-gallant-sails.

A SLIT is made up the middle of the sail from the foot, with a hole to go over the main-stay, and lace-holes on each side to lace it together when in its place.

To find the quantity of canvas, refer to Rule I. page 30.

TABLES

OF THE

DIMENSIONS OF ALL SAILS,

AND

THE QUANTITIES OF CANVAS

CONTAINED

IN EVERY PART OF EACH SAIL, WITH THE SORTS OF CANVAS OF WHICH THEY ARE RESPECTIVELY MADE,

FOR

Ships of all Rates.

OBSERVATIONS.

THE Canvas which is used for the Royal Navy is twenty-four inches wide; and it is certainly the strongest. This is the width by which the following Tables are calculated.

There are eight different sorts of this Canvas; of which the weight ⅌ bolt, or piece, of 38 yards is as follows:—No. 1, 44 ℔. No. 2, 41 ℔. No. 3, 38 ℔. No. 4, 35 ℔. No. 5, 32 ℔. No. 6, 29 ℔. No. 7, 24 ℔. and No. 8, 21 ℔.

DIMENSIONS OF THE SAILS, AND QUANTITY OF CANVAS

Contained in every Part of each Sail, with the Sorts of Canvas of which they are respectively made, for

A SHIP OF 100 GUNS, OR 2164 TONS.

NAMES OF THE SAILS.	Cloths Head	Cloths Foot	Yards Deep	Reef-Bands	Leech-Linings	Buntlings	Gores	Clue-Pieces	Reef-Tackle Pieces	Sort of Canvas	Total Yards
Sprit-Course	31	31	9¼	....	....	....	....	....	....	2	286¾
Top-Sail	20½	31	10½	....	....	....	....	....	....	6	270¾
Flying-Jib	....	16	19½	....	....	....	20	2	....	8	178
Jib	....	27	26	....	....	....	26⅔	4	....	6	381⅔
Fore-Course	42	40	12¼	17	28	16¼	10¾	....	....	1	574
Middle-Band	....	....	....	....	....	....	....	....	....	2	12¼
Foot do.	....	....	....	....	....	....	....	....	....	2	11⅓
Top-Sail	26½	43	19	38	40	11¼	....	....	5¼	2	731½
Top-Lining	....	....	....	....	....	....	....	....	....	5	61¼
Foot-Band	....	....	....	....	....	....	....	....	....	3	11¼
Middle do.	....	....	....	....	....	....	....	....	....	3	9⅓
Top-Gallant-Sail	20	27	9½	....	....	....	....	....	....	6	223½
Royal	12	20	7	....	....	....	....	....	....	7	112
Main-Course	48	50	14¾	19¾	34½	20	18	....	....	1	814⅗
Foot-Band	....	....	....	....	....	....	....	....	....	2	14⅔
Middle do.	....	....	....	....	....	....	....	....	....	2	15¼
Top-Sail	30½	48½	21	44	44	12	....	....	5¼	2	912¼
Top-Lining	....	....	....	....	....	....	....	....	....	5	74
Foot-Band	....	....	....	....	....	....	....	....	....	3	10¾
Middle do.	....	....	....	....	....	....	....	....	....	3	12¾
Top-Gallant-Sail	23	31	10½	....	....	....	....	....	....	6	283⅓
Royal	14	23	7½	....	....	....	....	....	....	7	138¾
Mizen-Course	17	18	10 20	3¾	....	....	11⅓	7	....	2	282¼
Top-Sail	21	31½	14¼ 15	22½	31½	9½	4	....	5¼	4	438⅝
Top-Lining	....	....	....	....	....	....	....	....	....	6	37¾
Foot-Band	....	....	....	....	....	....	....	....	....	5	8⅓
Middle do.	....	....	....	....	....	....	....	....	....	5	7
Top-Gallant-Sail	16	21½	6¾ 7½	....	....	....	4	....	....	7	120½
Royal	9½	16	5¼	....	....	....	....	....	....	8	66 11/12
Stay-Sails, Fore	....	23	12¼	9¾	....	....	....	2	....	1	152⅜
Fore-Top	....	22	19	....	....	....	....	2	....	5	211
Main	....	32	14¾	13⅓	....	....	....	2	....	1	261½
Main-Top	26	28	10 26	....	....	....	....	8¼	....	5	486¼
Main-Top-Gallant	22	22	7 16½	....	....	....	....	6½	....	7	265
Middle	25	25	8 17½	....	....	....	....	7	....	6	325¾
Mizen	23	25	8½ 14	....	....	....	....	7½	....	2	274¾
Mizen-Top	20	21	7 16	....	....	....	....	6½	....	6	240
Royal	18	18	5 11	....	....	....	....	5½	....	8	149½
Studding-Sails, Fore	19	19	15	....	....	....	....	....	....	6	285
Fore-Top	15	19	20	....	....	....	....	....	....	6	340
Fore-Top-Gallant	11	15	10	....	....	....	....	....	....	7	130
Main	20	20	18	3¼	....	....	....	....	....	6	363¼
Main-Top	16	20	22	2¾	....	....	....	....	....	6	398¾
Main-Top-Gallant	12	16	11	....	....	....	....	....	....	7	154
Driver	24	30	9½ 21	....	....	....	56	6	....	5	473¾
Try-Sail	8½	15	9½ 12½	11	....	....	12	13	....	1	165¼

DIMENSIONS OF THE SAILS, AND QUANTITY OF CANVAS

Contained in every Part of each Sail, with the Sorts of Canvas of which they are respectively made, for

A SHIP OF 90 GUNS, OR 1870 TONS.

NAMES OF THE SAILS.	Cloths: Head	Cloths: Foot	Yards Deep	Reef-Bands	Leech-Linings	Buntlings	Gores	Clue-Pieces	Reef-Tackle Pieces	Sort of Canvas	Total Yards
Sprit-Course	29	29	9	....	....	....	....	....	....	2	261
Top-Sail	19	29	10	....	....	....	....	....	....	6	240
Flying-Jib	....	15	18¾	....	....	....	18	2	....	8	160⅝
Jib	....	26	25	....	....	....	24½	4	....	6	353½
Fore-Course	40	38	11⅜	16	27	15⅓	10¾	....	....	1	524$\frac{1}{12}$
Middle-Band	....	....	....	....	....	....	....	....	....	2	12
Foot do.	....	....	....	....	....	....	....	....	....	2	10½
Top-Sail	26	41	18	37½	38	10¾	....	....	5¼	2	678¼
Top-Lining	....	....	....	....	....	....	....	....	....	5	58
Foot-Band	....	....	....	....	....	....	....	....	....	3	8¾
Middle do.	....	....	....	....	....	....	....	....	....	3	10¾
Top-Gallant-Sail	19	26	8¾	....	....	....	....	....	....	6	196¾
Royal	11	19½	6⅓	....	....	....	....	....	....	7	98⅙
Main-Course	46	48	13¾	19	31½	18⅓	14	....	....	1	729$\frac{1}{12}$
Foot-Band	....	....	....	....	....	....	....	....	....	2	13¾
Middle do.	....	....	....	....	....	....	....	....	....	2	14¼
Top-Sail	30	47½	20	43	42	12	....	....	5¼	2	855¾
Top-Lining	....	....	....	....	....	....	....	....	....	5	69¾
Foot-Band	....	....	....	....	....	....	....	....	....	3	10½
Middle do.	....	....	....	....	....	....	....	....	....	3	12½
Top-Gallant-Sail	21½	30	10	....	....	....	....	....	....	6	257½
Royal	13½	22	7⅓	....	....	....	....	....	....	7	130¼
Mizen-Course	16	17	9½ 19	3½	....	....	10	7	....	2	253¼
Top-Sail	21	29½	13¾ 14½	22	30½	9¼	4	....	5¼	4	412
Top-Lining	....	....	....	....	....	....	....	....	....	6	36⅜
Foot-Band	....	....	....	....	....	....	....	....	....	5	6¼
Middle do.	....	....	....	....	....	....	....	....	....	5	7¾
Top-Gallant-Sail	15	21½	6¼ 7	....	....	....	4	....	....	7	118
Royal	9	15	5½	....	....	....	....	....	....	8	61¼
Stay-Sails, Fore	....	22	11⅞	9⅛	....	....	....	2	....	1	139⅝
Fore-Top	....	21	18	....	....	....	....	2	....	5	191
Main	....	31	13¾	13	....	....	....	2	....	1	228⅛
Main-Top	25	27	9½ 25	....	....	....	....	8	....	5	448¾
Main-Top-Gallant	21	21	6½ 15½	....	....	....	....	6½	....	7	237½
Middle	24	24	7½ 16½	....	....	....	....	7	....	6	295
Mizen	22	24	8 13½	....	....	....	....	7	....	2	251⅓
Mizen-Top	19	20	6½ 15½	....	....	....	....	6½	....	6	218¾
Royal	17	17	4½ 10¾	....	....	....	....	5	....	8	134⅝
Studding-Sails, Fore	18	18	14½	....	....	....	....	....	....	6	261
Fore-Top	14	18	19	....	....	....	....	....	....	6	304
Fore-Top-Gallant	10	14	9¼	....	....	....	....	....	....	7	111
Main	19	19	17½	3¼	....	....	....	....	....	6	335¾
Main-Top	15	19	21	....	....	....	....	....	....	6	359½
Main-Top-Gallant	11	15	10½	....	....	....	....	....	...	7	136½
Driver	24	30	9 19¾	....	....	....	57	6	....	5	451⅛
Try-Sail	8	14½	9 12	....	....	....	11½	11½	....	1	152⅝

DIMENSIONS OF THE SAILS, AND QUANTITY OF CANVAS

Contained in every Part of each Sail, with the Sorts of Canvas of which they are respectively made, for

A SHIP OF 80 GUNS, OR 1920 TONS.

NAMES OF THE SAILS.	Cloths Head	Cloths Foot	Yards Deep	Reef-Bands	Leech-Linings	Buntlings	Gores	Clue-Pieces	Reef-Tackle Pieces	Sort of Canvas	Total Yards
Sprit-Course	31	31	9	....	....	....	....	....	....	2	279
Top-Sail	18	31	10½	....	....	....	....	....	....	6	257¼
Flying Jib	....	16	19½	....	....	....	20	2	....	8	178
Jib	....	27	26	....	....	....	26¾	4	....	6	381¾
Fore-Course	43	41	15	17½	34½	20	10½	....	....	1	712½
Middle-Band	....	....	....	....	....	....	....	....	....	2	12½
Foot do.	....	....	....	....	....	....	....	....	....	2	11⅞
Top-Sail	28	44	19	41	40	11½	....	....	5½	2	761
Top-Lining	....	....	....	....	....	....	....	....	....	5	61⅞
Foot-Band	....	....	....	....	....	....	....	....	....	3	9⅞
Middle do.	....	....	....	....	....	....	....	....	....	3	11¼
Top-Gallant-Sail	18	28	9½	....	....	....	....	....	....	6	212¾
Royal	11	18½	6¾	....	....	....	....	....	....	7	98¼
Main-Course	49¼	51½	16½	20½	37¼	21½	18	....	....	1	922 7/12
Foot-Band	....	....	....	....	....	....	....	....	....	2	14½
Middle do.	....	....	....	....	....	....	....	....	....	2	15¼
Top-Sail	32	50½	21	....	....	....	....	....	....	2	952
Top-Lining	....	....	....	....	....	....	....	....	....	5	74
Foot-Band	....	....	....	....	....	....	....	....	....	3	11¼
Middle do.	....	....	....	....	....	....	....	....	....	3	13¼
Top-Gallant-Sail	21½	32	10½	....	....	....	....	....	....	6	280 7/12
Royal	13½	22	7¾	....	....	....	....	....	....	7	136
Mizen-Course	17	18	12½ 23	3½	....	....	11½	7	....	2	329½
Top-Sail	22	31½	14½ 15½	23	32	9⅝	4	....	5¼	4	454½
Top-Lining	....	....	....	....	....	....	....	....	....	6	39¾
Foot-Band	....	....	....	....	....	....	....	....	....	5	7
Middle do.	....	....	....	....	....	....	....	....	....	5	8¼
Top-Gallant-Sail	16	22½	6¾ 7½	....	....	....	4	....	....	7	134
Royal	9½	16	5¼	....	....	....	....	....	....	8	70½
Stay-Sails, Fore	....	22	15	9⅝	....	....	....	2	....	1	176¼
Fore-Top	....	21	19	....	....	....	....	2	....	5	201½
Main	....	32	16½	13½	....	....	....	2	....	1	276⅝
Main-Top	26	28	10 25	....	....	....	....	8½	....	5	473½
Main-Top-Gallant	22	22	7 16½	....	....	....	....	6½	....	7	265½
Middle	25	25	7¼ 15½	....	....	....	....	7	....	6	297¼
Mizen	20½	22½	9 13½	....	....	....	....	7½	....	2	246½
Mizen-Top	20	21	7 16	....	....	....	....	6½	....	6	240¼
Royal	18	18	5 11⅓	....	....	....	....	5¼	....	8	152¼
Studding-Sails, Fore	18	18	17	....	....	....	....	....	....	6	306
Fore-Top	14	18	20	....	....	....	....	....	....	6	320
Fore-Top-Gallant	10	14	9¾	....	....	....	....	....	....	7	117
Main	19	19	19½	3½	....	....	....	....	....	6	370¾
Main-Top	15	19	22	....	....	....	....	....	....	6	376¼
Main-Top-Gallant	11	15	11	....	....	....	....	....	....	7	143
Driver	25	33	11¼ 24	....	....	....	65½	6	....	5	590¼
Try-Sail	8½	15	11½ 14½	11	....	....	12	14	....	1	189¼

DIMENSIONS OF THE SAILS, AND QUANTITY OF CANVAS

Contained in every Part of each Sail, with the Sorts of Canvas of which they are respectively made, for

A SHIP OF 74 GUNS, OR 1800 TONS.

NAMES OF THE SAILS.	Cloths		Yards Deep	Reef-Bands	Leech-Linings	Buntlings	Gores	Clue-Pieces	Reef-Tackle Pieces	Sort of Canvas	Total Yards
	Head	Foot									
Sprit-Course	30	30	8⅓							2	255
Top-Sail	19	30	10							6	245
Flying Jib		15	18¾				18	2		8	160⅝
Jib		27	26				26⅔	4		6	381⅓
Fore-Course	41	39	13⅓	16¾	30	17¾	10¾			1	608 7/12
Foot-Band										2	11
Middle do.										2	12¼
Top-Sail	27	42	18	38¾	38	10¾			5¼	2	696¼
Foot-Band										3	9
Middle do.										3	11
Top-Lining										5	58
Top-Gallant-Sail	19	27	9							6	207
Royal	11½	19½	6½							7	100¾
Main-Course	47	49	15¾	19¾	35¼	21	14			1	846¼
Foot-Band											14¼
Middle do.											14¾
Top-Sail	13	48	20½	43¾	42⅓	12⅓			5¼	2	882⅓
Foot-Band										3	10¼
Middle do.										3	12¾
Top-Lining										5	72½
Top-Gallant-Sail	21½	31	10							6	262½
Royal	13½	22	7½							7	133½
Mizen-Course	16	17	11 21	3½			10	7		2	282
Top-Sail	20½	30½	14¼ 15	22¼	31½	10	4		5¼	4	431¼
Foot-Band										5	6¼
Middle do.										5	8
Top-Lining										6	38¼
Top-Gallant-Sail	15	21½	6¾ 7½				4			7	127⅛
Royal	9	15	5⅓							8	64
Stay-Sails, Fore		22	13⅓	9¼				2		1	157 11/12
Fore-Top		21	18					2		5	191
Main		32	15¾	13½				2		1	267½
Main-Top	25	27	9½ 25					8		5	448¾
Main-Top-Gallant	21	21	6½ 15½					6⅓		7	237⅓
Middle	24	24	7½ 16½					7		6	295
Mizen	20½	22½	9 13½					7½		2	246½
Mizen-Top	19	20	6½ 15½					6⅓		6	218¾
Royal	17	17	4½ 10¾					5¼		8	134⅞
Studding-Sails, Fore	18	18	15⅓							6	276
Fore-Top	14	18	19							6	304
Fore-Top-Gallant	10	14	9½							7	114
Main	19	19	18¾	3½						6	359½
Main-Top	15	19	21¼	2½						6	363¾
Main-Top-Gallant	11	15	10½							7	136½
Driver	25	31⅓	10½ 21¼			60	6			5	514½
Try-Sail	8	14⅓	10½ 13	10⅓		12½	12½			1	167⅜

DIMENSIONS OF THE SAILS, AND QUANTITY OF CANVAS

Contained in every Part of each Sail, with the Sorts of Canvas of which they are respectively made, for

A SHIP OF 64 GUNS, or 1569 TONS.

NAMES OF THE SAILS.	Cloths		Yards Deep	Reef-Bands	Leech-Linings	Buntlings	Gores	Clue-Pieces	Reef-Tackle Pieces	Sort of Canvas	Total Yards
	Head	Foot									
Sprit-Course	27	27	7½							2	202½
Top-Sail	16	27	9							6	193½
Flying Jib		14	17¼				16	2		8	138¾
Jib		25	24				22½	2		6	326½
Fore-Course	38	36	12	15¼	26½	16	8			1	509¾
Foot-Band										2	10
Middle do.										2	11
Top-Sail	24½	38½	16	35	34	9¾			5¼	2	574½
Foot-Band										3	8⅛
Middle do.										3	10
Top-Lining										5	47½
Top-Gallant-Sail	16	25	8							6	164
Royal	10	16½	5¾							7	76¼
Main-Course	43	45	14	17¾	31	18⅜	10¾			1	694⅛
Foot-Band										2	12¾
Middle do.										2	13¾
Top-Sail	28	44	18	40¾	38	10¾			5¼	2	726¾
Foot-Band										3	9¾
Middle do.										3	11¾
Top-Lining										5	58
Top-Gallant-Sail	18	28½	9							6	209¼
Royal	11	18½	6½							7	95⅞
Mizen-Course	15	16	9½ 18	3¼		9	9½	7		2	230¾
Top-Sail	19	28	12¼ 13	20	27½	8¼	4		5¼	4	247½
Foot-Band										5	5¾
Middle do.										5	7¼
Top-Lining										6	29
Top-Gallant-Sail	13½	19½	5¾ 6½				4			7	98⅞
Royal	8½	14	4¾							8	53⅓
Stay-Sails, Fore		20	12	8½				2		1	130⅓
Fore-Top		19	16					2		5	154
Main		29	14	12¼				2		1	217¼
Main-Top	22	24	9 22½					7½		5	363
Main-Top-Gallant	18	18	5 14					5½		7	176⅓
Middle	21	21	6 13½					6		6	210¾
Mizen	20	22	8 12					7		2	215
Mizen-Top	16	17	5 13½					5½		6	156
Royal	14	14	4¼ 9					5		8	97½
Studding-Sails, Fore	16	16	14							6	224
Fore-Top	12	16	17							6	238
Fore-Top-Gallant	9	12	8½							7	89¼
Main	17	17	17	2¾						6	291¾
Main-Top	13	17	19	2¼						6	287½
Main-Top-Gallant	10	13	9½							7	109¼
Driver	22½	28	9 19				51	6		5	411⅓
Try-Sail	7	13½	9 11½	9½			11½	11½		1	137⅓

DIMENSIONS OF THE SAILS, AND QUANTITY OF CANVAS

Contained in every Part of each Sail, with the Sorts of Canvas of which they are respectively made, for

A SHIP OF 50 GUNS, OR 1444 TONS.

NAMES OF THE SAILS.	Cloths: Head	Cloths: Foot	Yards Deep	Reef-Bands	Leech-Linings	Buntlings	Gores	Clue-Pieces	Reef-Tackle Pieces	Sort of Canvas	Total Yards
Sprit-Course	25	25	7							2	175
Top-Sail	14½	25	8							6	158
Flying Jib		13	15¾				15	2		8	119⅜
Jib		22	21				16¾	4		6	251¾
Fore-Course	34½	33½	11	13¾	25	14¾	6			1	433½
Foot-Band										2	9¼
Middle do.										2	10
Top-Sail	22½	35½	14⅜	33	31¼	9			5¼	2	494¼
Foot-Band										3	7½
Middle do.										3	9¼
Top-Lining										5	43⅝
Top-Gallant-Sail	14½	23	7¼							6	135¾
Royal	9	15	5⅓							7	64
Main-Course	40	42	12½	16½	28½	16⅝	10½			1	584⅔
Foot-Band										2	11⅔
Middle do.										2	12½
Top-Sail	26	40½	16¼	38	34½	9⅝			5¼	2	615⅓
Foot-Band										3	8¾
Middle do.										3	10¾
Top-Lining										5	52⅔
Top-Gallant-Sail	17	26½	8							6	174
Royal	10½	17½	5¾							7	80½
Mizen-Course	13	14	8½ 16½	2¾			9	7		2	185½
Top-Sail	17½	25½	11¼ 12	18¼	25½	7¾	4		5¼	4	298
Foot-Band										5	5¼
Middle do.										5	6¾
Top-Lining										6	26⅔
Top-Gallant-Sail	12½	18	5½ 6				2¼			7	86⅛
Royal	7½	13	4½							8	46⅛
Stay-Sails, Fore		18	11	7⅓				2		1	108⅔
Fore-Top		17	15					2		5	129½
Main		26	12½	11				2		1	175½
Main-Top	21	23	8¾ 21¾					7¾		5	336¾
Main-Top-Gallant	17	17	4½ 13½					5½		7	158½
Middle	20	20	5½ 13					6		6	191
Mizen	18	20	7 12					6½		2	184½
Mizen-Top	15	16	4½ 13					5½		6	139
Royal	13	13	4 8½					5		8	86¼
Studding-Sails, Fore	15	15	13							6	195
Fore-Top	11	15	15¾							6	204¾
Fore-Top-Gallant	8	11	7¾							7	73⅝
Main	16	16	15	2¾						6	242¾
Main-Top	12	16	17¼	2¾						6	243¾
Main-Top-Gallant	9	12	8½							7	89¼
Driver	21	27	8 17				47	6		5	353
Try-Sail	6½	12	8 10½	8½			10	11		1	115

DIMENSIONS OF THE SAILS, AND QUANTITY OF CANVAS

Contained in every Part of each Sail, with the Sorts of Canvas of which they are respectively made, for

A SHIP OF 60 GUNS, OR 1500 TONS.

NAMES OF THE SAILS.	Cloths		Yards Deep	Reef-Bands	Leech-Linings	Buntlings	Gores	Clue-Pieces	Reef-Tackle Pieces	Sort of Canvas	Total Yards
	Head	Foot									
Sprit-Course	27	27	7½	....	....	....	....	....	....	2	202½
Top-Sail	16	27	9	....	....	....	....	....	....	6	193½
Flying-Jib	....	14	17¼	....	....	....	16	2	....	8	138¾
Jib	....	25	24	....	....	....	22½	4	....	6	326½
Fore-Course	38	36	12	15¼	26½	16	8	....	....	1	509¾
Middle-Band	....	....	....	....	....	....	....	....	....	2	11
Foot do.	....	....	....	....	....	....	....	....	....	2	10
Top-Sail	24½	38½	16	35	34	9¾	....	....	5¼	2	573½
Top-Lining	....	....	....	....	....	....	....	....	....	5	47½
Middle-Band	....	....	....	....	....	....	....	....	....	3	10
Foot do.	....	....	....	....	....	....	....	....	....	3	8½
Top-Gallant-Sail	16	25	8	....	....	....	....	....	....	6	164
Royal	10	16½	5¾	....	....	....	....	....	....	7	76¼
Main-Course	43	45	14	17¾	31	18⅜	10¾	....	....	1	694⅛
Middle-Band	....	....	....	....	....	....	....	....	....	2	13¾
Foot do.	....	....	....	....	....	....	....	....	....	2	12¾
Top-Sail	28	44	18	40¾	38	10¾	....	....	5¼	2	725¾
Top-Lining	....	....	....	....	....	....	....	....	....	5	58
Middle-Band	....	....	....	....	....	....	....	....	....	3	11¾
Foot do.	....	....	....	....	....	....	....	....	....	3	9¾
Top-Gallant-Sail	18	28½	9	....	....	....	....	....	....	6	209¼
Royal	11	18½	6½	....	....	....	....	....	....	7	95⅞
Mizen-Course	15	16	9½ 18	3¼	....	....	9½	7	....	2	230¾
Top-Sail	19	28	11¾ 13	20	27½	8¼	4	....	5¼	4	351¾
Top-Lining	....	....	....	....	....	....	....	....	....	6	29
Middle-Band	....	....	....	....	....	....	....	....	....	5	7¼
Foot do.	....	....	....	....	....	....	....	....	....	5	5⅝
Top-Gallant-Sail	13½	19½	5¾ 6½	....	....	....	4	....	....	7	98⅞
Royal	8½	14	4¾	....	....	....	....	....	....	8	53⅓
Stay-Sails, Fore	....	20	12	8½	....	....	....	2	....	1	130½
Main	....	29	14	12¼	....	....	....	2	....	1	217¼
Mizen	20	22	8 12	....	....	....	....	7	....	2	215
Main-Top	22	24	9 22½	....	....	....	....	7½	....	5	363
Fore-Top	....	19	16	....	....	....	....	2	....	5	154
Main-Top-Gallant	18	18	5 14	....	....	....	....	5½	....	7	176½
Mizen-Top	16	17	5 13½	....	....	....	....	5½	....	6	156
Middle	21	21	6 13½	....	....	....	....	6	....	6	210¾
Royal	14	14	4¼ 9	....	....	....	....	5	....	8	97¾
Studding-Sails, Main	17	17	17	2¾	....	....	....	....	....	6	291¾
Main-Top	13	17	19	2¾	....	....	....	....	....	6	287¼
Main-Top-Gallant	10	13	9½	....	....	....	....	....	....	7	109⅓
Fore	16	16	14	....	....	....	....	....	....	6	224
Fore-Top	12	16	17	....	....	....	....	....	....	6	238
Fore-Top-Gallant	9	12	8½	....	....	....	....	....	....	7	89¼
Driver	22½	28	9 19	....	....	....	51	6	....	5	411½
Try-Sail	7	13½	9 11½	....	....	....	11½	11½	....	1	137½

DIMENSIONS OF THE SAILS, AND QUANTITY OF CANVAS

Contained in every Part of each Sail, with the Sorts of Canvas of which they are respectively made, for

A SHIP OF 46 GUNS, OR 1200 TONS.

NAMES OF THE SAILS.	Cloths		Yards Deep	Reef-Bands	Leech-Linings	Buntlings	Gores	Clue-Pieces	Reef-Tackle Pieces	Sort of Canvas.	Total Yards
	Head	Foot									
Sprit-Course	25	25	7	....	....	....	....	....	....	3	175
Top Sail	15½	26	8½	....	....	....	....	....	....	7	176½
Flying-Jib	....	13	15	....	....	....	15	2	....	8	114½
Jib	....	21	20	....	....	....	15	4	....	7	229
Fore-Course	34½	33½	11¾	13¾	26	15¾	6	....	....	1	460 11/15
Middle-Band	....	....	....	....	....	....	....	....	....	2	10
Foot do.	....	....	....	....	....	....	....	....	....	2	9⅓
Top-Sail	23	35	14¾	33	31¼	9	....	....	5¼	3	496
Top-Lining	....	....	....	....	....	....	....	....	....	6	44⅓
Middle-Band	....	....	....	....	....	....	....	....	....	4	9¼
Foot do.	....	....	....	....	....	....	....	....	....	4	7½
Top-Gallant-Sail	15½	23½	7½	....	....	....	....	....	....	7	143
Royal	9½	16	5⅓	....	....	....	....	....	....	8	68
Main-Course	39½	41½	13¾	16⅓	30	18⅓	8	....	....	1	629½
Middle-Band	....	....	....	....	....	....	....	....	....	2	12½
Foot do.	....	....	....	....	....	....	....	....	....	2	11⅓
Top-Sail	26	40	16¾	38	36	10⅛	....	....	5¼	3	627⅔
Top-Lining	....	....	....	....	....	....	....	....	....	6	54⅔
Middle-Band	....	....	....	....	....	....	....	....	....	4	10⅓
Foot do.	....	....	....	....	....	....	....	....	....	4	9½
Top-Gallant-Sail	17	26½	8½	....	....	....	....	....	....	7	184⅞
Royal	10½	17½	6	....	....	....	....	....	....	8	84
Mizen-Course	13	14	11⅔ 20	3½	....	....	9	7	....	3	230⅔
Top-Sail	18	26	12 12¾	19	26½	8	4¼	....	2½	5	316
Top-Lining	....	....	....	....	....	....	....	....	....	7	28⅔
Middle-Band	....	....	....	....	....	....	....	....	....	6	6¾
Foot do.	....	....	....	....	....	....	....	....	....	6	5½
Top-Gallant-Sail	13½	19	5¾ 6¼	....	....	....	2¼	....	....	8	95⅛
Royal	8	14	4½	....	....	....	....	....	....	8	49½
Stay-Sails, Fore	....	17	11¾	7	....	....	....	2	....	2	108⅞
Main	....	24	13¾	10	....	....	....	2	....	2	177
Mizen	17	19	7 12	....	....	....	....	6½	....	3	175
Main-Top	19½	21½	8 20½	....	....	....	....	7½	....	6	295¾
Fore-Top	....	16	14¾	....	....	....	....	2	....	6	120
Main-Top-Gallant	15	15	4⅓ 12	....	....	....	....	5⅓	....	7	129¼
Mizen-Top	13	14	4 12	....	....	....	....	5	....	7	111
Middle	18	18	5½ 10½	....	....	....	....	6	....	7	150
Royal	11	11	4 8½	....	....	....	....	5	....	8	73¾
Studding-Sails, Main	14	14	15¾	2½	....	....	....	....	....	7	223
Main-Top	11	14	17¾	2	....	....	....	....	....	7	223⅞
Main-Top-Gallant	8	11	9	....	....	....	....	....	....	8	85½
Fore	13	13	13¼	....	....	....	....	....	....	7	172¼
Fore-Top	10	13	15¾	....	....	....	....	....	....	7	181⅛
Fore-Top-Gallant	7	10	7¾	....	....	....	....	....	....	8	65⅞
Driver	20½	27	11¼ 20½	....	....	....	47	6	....	5	430
Try-Sail	6½	12	11 13	8½	....	....	10	12¾	....	1	142¼

DIMENSIONS OF THE SAILS, AND QUANTITY OF CANVAS

Contained in every Part of each Sail, with the Sorts of Canvas of which they are respectively made, for

A SHIP OF 36 GUNS, OR 900 TONS.

NAMES OF THE SAILS.	Cloths Head	Cloths Foot	Yards Deep	Reef-Bands	Leech-Linings	Buntlings	Gores	Clue-Pieces	Reef-Tackle Pieces	Sort of Canvas	Total Yards
Sprit-Course	24	24	7							3	168
Top-Sail	15	25	8¼							7	165
Flying-Jib		13	15				15	2		8	114½
Jib		21	20				15	4		7	229
Fore-Course	33	32	11¼	13½	27	16½	6			1	461
Middle-Band										2	8¾
Foot do.										2	9½
Top-Sail	22	34	14¼	31½	30½	9			5½	3	437
Top-Lining										6	39½
Middle-Band										4	9¼
Foot do.										4	7½
Top-Gallant-Sail	15	23	7½							7	137¾
Royal	9½	15	5¼							8	64¼
Main-Course	38	40	13½	16	29¼	17½	8			1	587½
Middle-Band										2	12
Foot do.										2	11¼
Top-Sail	25	39	16½	36¾	34¼	9¼			5½	3	599
Top-Lining										6	49¾
Middle-Band										4	10⅜
Foot do.										4	9⅓
Top-Gallant-Sail	17¼	25¼	8¼							7	177⅞
Royal	11½	18	6							8	88½
Mizen-Course	13	14	11 18½	2¾			9	7		3	216
Top-Sail	17½	25½	11½ 12¼	18½	26	6¾	4		2½	5	300
Top-Lining										7	27¼
Middle-Band										6	6¾
Foot do.										6	5¼
Top-Gallant-Sail	13	18	5¾ 6¼					2½		8	91⅞
Royal	8½	13½	4½							8	49¼
Stay-Sails, Fore		17	12½	7				2		2	113¾
Main		24	13½	10				2		2	174
Mizen	17	19	7 12					6½		3	175
Main-Top	20	22	8 20½					7¼		6	300¼
Fore-Top		16	14½					2		6	118
Main-Top-Gallant	15	15	4½ 11½					5½		7	125¼
Mizen-Top	13	14	4 12					5		7	111
Middle	18	18	5½ 11					5⅝		7	152½
Royal	11	11	3¾ 8½					5		8	71
Studding-Sails, Main	14	14	15½	2½						7	216¾
Main-Top	11	14	17½	2						7	220¼
Main-Top-Gallant	8	11	8¾							8	83¼
Fore	13	13	14							7	182
Fore-Top	10	13	15½							7	178½
Fore-Top-Gallant	7	10	7¾							8	65¼
Driver	20	26	10½ 20				45	6		5	401¼
Try-Sail	6	12	10½ 12½	8½			10	12½		1	134½

DIMENSIONS OF THE SAILS, AND QUANTITY OF CANVAS

Contained in every Part of each Sail, with the Sorts of Canvas of which they are respectively made, for

A SHIP OF 32 GUNS, or 680 TONS.

NAMES OF THE SAILS.	Cloths Head	Cloths Foot	Yards Deep	Reef-Bands	Leech-Linings	Buntlings	Gores	Reef-Tackle Pieces	Clue-Pieces	Sort of Canvas	Total Yards
Sprit-Course	23	23	6½							3	149½
Top-Sail	13½	23	7¼							7	141¼
Flying-Jib		12	14½				12		2	8	99½
Jib		20	19				13¾		3	7	206⅞
Fore-Course	30½	29½	11	12	24½	14¾	6			1	387⅛
Foot-Band										2	8
Middle do.										2	9
Top-Sail	20½	31	13¾	13¼	30	28½	8¾	5¼		3	418
Foot-Band										4	6⅜
Middle do.										4	8½
Top-Lining										6	35½
Top-Gallant-Sail	13½	21	6¾							7	116⅜
Royal	8½	14	5							8	56¼
Main-Course	35	37	13	14½	29	17½	8			1	536⅝
Foot-Band										2	10¼
Middle do.										2	11½
Top-Sail	23½	36	15½	33½	32½	9½		5¼		3	531¼
Foot-Band										4	8
Middle do.										4	9½
Top-Lining										6	42 1/12
Top-Gallant-Sail	15½	24	7¾							7	153¼
Royal	9½	16	5¾							8	72¼
Mizen-Course	11	11	10 18	2½			7		7	3	163
Top-Sail	16	23½	11 11¾	17	24½	7½	4	2½		5	268½
Foot-Band										6	:5
Middle do.										6	6
Top-Lining										7	23
Top-Gallant-Sail	11½	17	5¼ 5¾					2¼		8	77
Royal	7	12	4½							8	40
Stay-Sails, Fore		16	11	6¾					2	2	96¾
Fore-Top		15	13½						2	6	105¼
Main		23	13	9½					2	2	161
Main-Top	19	21	8 20½						7	6	286
Main-Top-Gallant	14	14	3½ 11½						5	7	110
Royal	10	10	3¾ 8½						5	8	65
Middle	17	17	4½ 11½						5½	7	141½
Mizen	15	17	6½ 11½						6½	3	148
Mizen-Top	12	13	3½ 11½						5	7	96¼
Studding-Sails, Fore	12	12	12¼							7	153
Fore-Top	9	12	14¾							7	154¾
Fore-Top-Gallant	6	9	7¼							8	54¾
Main	13	13	15	2¼						7	197¾
Main-Top	10	13	16½	1¾						7	191½
Main-Top-Gallant	7	10	8¼							8	70½
Driver	19	24½	9½ 18				33½		6	5	338 11/12
Try-Sail	5½	10	9½ 11	7½			8		11½	1	106¼

DIMENSIONS OF THE SAILS, AND QUANTITY OF CANVAS

Contained in every Part of each Sail, with the Sorts of Canvas of which they are respectively made, for

A SHIP OF 28 GUNS, OR 600 TONS.

NAMES OF THE SAILS.	Cloths Head	Cloths Foot	Yards Deep	Reef-Bands	Leech-Linings	Buntlings	Gores	Reef-Tackle Pieces	Clue-Pieces	Sort of Canvas	Total Yards
Sprit-Course	22	22	6¼							3	137½
Top-Sail	13	22	7½							7	131¼
Flying-Jib		11	13½				9		2	8	85¼
Jib		19	18				12⅝		3	7	186⅝
Fore-Course	29½	28½	10¼	11½	22¾	13⅝	6			1	351¼
Foot-Band										2	7⅝
Middle do.										2	8¾
Top-Sail	19½	20	13	28½	27½	8		5¼		3	384 1/12
Foot-Band										4	6⅓
Middle do.										4	7¾
Top-Lining										6	31⅛
Top-Gallant-Sail	13	20	6⅓							7	107¼
Royal	8	13½	4¾							8	51¼
Main-Course	33½	35½	12½	13½	28	16⅝	8			1	497⅝
Foot-Band										2	9⅝
Middle do.										2	10⅛
Top-Sail	22⅓	34½	14¾	33	31	9		5¼		3	489¼
Foot-Band										4	7½
Middle do.										4	9⅛
Top-Lining										6	40¼
Top-Gallant-Sail	15	23	7½							7	142½
Royal	9	15½	5⅓							8	65½
Mizen-Course	10	11	9½ 17	2¼			7		7	3	153½
Top-Sail	15½	22	10½ 11¼	16¼	23½	7	4	2½		5	246 1/12
Foot-Band										6	4½
Middle do.										6	5¾
Top-Lining										7	21¾
Top-Gallant-Sail	11	16	5¼ 5¾					2¼		8	73⅛
Royal	7	11½	4							8	37
Stay-Sails, Fore		16	10¼	6⅝					2	2	90⅝
Fore-Top		15	13						2	6	99½
Main		23	12½	9½					2	2	155¼
Main-Top	19	21	8 20½						7	6	286
Main-Top-Gallant	14	14	3½ 11½						5	7	110
Royal	10	10	3½ 8						5	8	62½
Middle	17	17	4½ 11½						5½	7	141½
Mizen	15	17	6 11						6	3	139½
Mizen-Top	12	13	3½ 11½						5	7	96¾
Studding-Sails, Fore	11	11	12							7	132
Fore-Top	8	11	14							7	133
Fore-Top-Gallant	5	8	7							8	45
Main	12	12	14⅓							7	170¼
Main-Top	9	12	15¾							7	167⅞
Main-Top-Gallant	6	9	8							8	60
Driver	18	24	9 17½				30			5	313¼
Try-Sail	5	10	9 10½				7¼			1	99⅝

DIMENSIONS OF THE SAILS, AND QUANTITY OF CANVAS

Contained in every Part of each Sail, with the Sorts of Canvas of which they are respectively made, for

A SHIP OF 24 GUNS, OR 520 TONS.

NAMES OF THE SAILS.	Cloths		Yards Deep	Reef-Bands	Leech-Linings	Buntlings	Gores	Reef-Tackle Pieces	Clue-Pieces	Sort of Canvas	Total Yards
	Head	Foot									
Sprit-Course	19	19	6	....	....	....	....	....	....	3	114
Top-Sail	12½	20	6¾	....	....	....	....	....	....	7	109⅔
Flying-Jib	....	11	13½	....	....	....	9	....	2	8	85¼
Jib	....	19	18	....	....	....	12⅔	....	3	7	186⅔
Fore-Course	27	26	9	10⅔	20	12	4	....	....	1	285⅓
Foot-Band	....	....	....	....	....	....	....	....	....	2	6¾
Middle do.	....	....	....	....	....	....	....	....	....	2	7¾
Top-Sail	17½	27½	12⅓	25¾	26	7¾	....	5¼	....	3	336⅓
Foot-Band	....	....	....	....	....	....	....	....	....	4	6
Middle do.	....	....	....	....	....	....	....	....	....	4	7¼
Top-Lining	....	....	....	....	....	....	....	....	....	6	26⅔
Top-Gallant-Sail	12½	18	6	....	....	....	....	....	....	7	91½
Royal	7½	13	4½	....	....	....	....	....	....	8	46⅛
Main-Course	31	33	10⅔	12¾	23¾	14¼	6½	....	....	1	$398\frac{7}{12}$
Foot-Band	....	....	....	....	....	....	....	....	....	2	9
Middle do.	....	....	....	....	....	....	....	....	....	2	9¾
Top-Sail	20	31½	13¾	29¼	28½	7¾	....	5¼	....	3	417⅝
Foot-Band	....	....	....	....	....	....	....	....	....	4	8¼
Middle do.	....	....	....	....	....	....	....	....	....	4	7
Top-Lining	....	....	....	....	....	....	....	....	....	6	33⅝
Top-Gallant-Sail	14	20½	6¾	....	....	....	....	....	....	7	116½
Royal	8½	14½	5	....	....	....	....	....	....	8	57½
Mizen-Course	10	10	8½ 15½	2	....	6	....	....	6	3	134
Top-Sail	14	20	9¼ 10	14¾	21	6⅓	....	2⅓	....	5	$201\frac{1}{12}$
Foot-Band	....	....	....	....	....	....	....	....	....	6	5¼
Middle do.	....	....	....	....	....	....	....	....	....	6	4
Top-Lining	....	....	....	....	....	....	....	....	....	7	16½
Top-Gallant-Sail	10	14½	4¾ 5¼	....	....	2¼	....	....	....	8	$60\frac{5}{12}$
Royal	6	10½	3⅔	....	....	....	....	....	....	8	30¼
Stay-Sails, Fore	....	14	9	6	....	....	....	....	2	2	71
Fore-Top	....	13	12⅓	....	....	....	....	....	2	6	82⅙
Main	....	22	10⅔	9¼	....	....	....	....	2	2	$128\frac{7}{12}$
Main-Top	17	19	7 18	....	....	....	....	....	6½	6	226
Main-Top-Gallant	13	13	2¾ 10¼	....	....	....	....	....	4¼	7	89
Royal	9	9	3¼ 7	....	....	....	....	....	4¾	8	50⅞
Middle	16	16	4¼ 10¾	....	....	....	....	....	5¼	7	125¼
Mizen	14	15	5 10½	....	....	....	....	....	5½	3	116⅓
Mizen-Top	11	12	3 10½	....	....	....	....	....	4¾	7	80½
Studding-Sails, Fore	11	11	10¾	....	....	....	....	....	....	7	118¼
Fore-Top	8	11	13⅓	....	....	....	....	....	....	7	126⅔
Fore-Top-Gallant	5	8	6½	....	....	....	....	....	....	8	42¼
Main	12	12	12⅔	2	....	....	....	....	....	7	154
Main-Top	9	12	14¾	1½	....	....	....	....	....	7	156⅜
Main-Top-Gallant	6	9	7¼	....	....	....	....	....	....	8	54½
Driver	16	22	8 15½	....	....	....	25	....	6	5	254¼
Try-Sail	4½	8½	8 9¼	6½	....	....	6¾	....	10⅓	1	$79\frac{7}{12}$

DIMENSIONS OF THE SAILS, AND QUANTITY OF CANVAS

Contained in every Part of each Sail, with the Sorts of Canvas of which they are respectively made, for

A SHIP OF 20 GUNS, or 430 TONS.

NAMES OF THE SAILS.	Cloths Head	Cloths Foot	Yards Deep	Reef-Bands	Leech-Linings	Buntlings	Gores	Reef-Tackle Pieces	Clue-Pieces	Sort of Canvas	Total Yards
Sprit-Course	19	19	5¼	....	....	....	....	....	....	3	104½
Top-Sail	11½	19½	6¾	....	....	....	....	....	....	7	103⅝
Flying-Jib	....	10	12	....	....	....	7	....	2	8	69
Jib	....	17	16	....	....	....	10¼	....	3	7	149¼
Fore-Course	26	25	9	10½	20	12	4	....	....	1	276
Foot-Band	....	....	....	....	....	....	....	....	....	2	6½
Middle do.	....	....	....	....	....	....	....	....	....	2	7½
Top-Sail	17	26½	11⅜	25	24½	7½	....	5¼	....	3	310
Foot-Band	....	....	....	....	....	....	....	....	....	4	5¾
Middle do.	....	....	....	....	....	....	....	....	....	4	6¾
Top-Lining	....	....	....	....	....	....	....	....	....	6	25 5/12
Top-Gallant-Sail	11½	18	5¾	....	....	....	....	....	....	7	84¾
Royal	7	12	4½	....	....	....	....	....	....	8	40½
Main-Course	30	32	10¼	12½	23	13¾	6	....	....	1	372⅜
Foot-Band	....	....	....	....	....	....	....	....	....	2	8½
Middle do.	....	....	....	....	....	....	....	....	....	2	9½
Top-Sail	19½	30½	13¼	28½	27½	8½	....	5¼	....	3	392⅝
Foot-Band	....	....	....	....	....	....	....	....	....	4	6⅝
Middle do.	....	....	....	....	....	....	....	....	....	4	8
Top-Lining	....	....	....	....	....	....	....	....	....	6	32½
Top-Gallant-Sail	13	20	6¾	....	....	....	....	....	....	7	110
Royal	8	13½	4¾	....	....	....	....	....	....	8	51
Mizen-Course	9½	9½	8 14½	2	....	....	5¼	....	6	3	120¼
Top-Sail	13½	19½	9¼ 10	14½	21	6⅜	4	2½	....	5	195¼
Foot-Band	....	....	....	....	....	....	....	....	....	6	4
Middle do.	....	....	....	....	....	....	....	....	....	6	5¼
Top-Lining	....	....	....	....	....	....	....	....	....	7	16½
Top-Gallant-Sail	10	14	4½ 5	....	....	....	2½	....	....	8	56½
Royal	6	10	3 2⅜	....	....	....	....	....	....	8	29¼
Stay-Sails, Fore	....	14	9	6	....	....	....	....	2	2	71
Fore-Top	....	13	11¾	....	....	....	....	....	2	6	77¾
Main	....	21	10¼	9	....	....	....	....	2	2	118⅜
Main-Top	17	19	7 18	....	....	....	....	....	6½	6	226
Main-Top-Gallant	13	13	2¾ 10¼	....	....	....	....	....	4½	7	89
Royal	9	9	3 6½	....	....	....	....	....	4½	8	48⅜
Middle	16	16	4¼ 10¾	....	....	....	....	....	5¼	7	125¼
Mizen	14	15	5 10	....	....	....	....	....	5½	3	113
Mizen-Top	11	12	3 10½	....	....	....	....	....	4¾	7	80½
Studding-Sails, Fore	10	10	10¼	....	....	....	....	....	....	7	107¼
Fore-Top	7	10	12¾	....	....	....	....	....	....	7	107¾
Fore-Top-Gallant	5	7	6½	....	....	....	....	....	....	8	37½
Main	11	11	12	2	....	....	....	....	....	7	134
Main-Top	8	11	14½	1½	....	....	....	....	....	7	136¼
Main-Top-Gallant	6	8	7½	....	....	....	....	....	....	8	50¼
Driver	15½	21	7½ 15	....	....	....	24	....	6	6	235¼
Try-Sail	4½	8½	8 9¼	6½	....	....	6¼	....	10⅜	1	79 7/12

DIMENSIONS OF THE SAILS, AND QUANTITY OF CANVAS

Contained in every Part of each Sail, with the Sorts of Canvas of which they are respectively made, for

A SLOOP OF 422 TONS.

NAMES OF THE SAILS.	Cloths Head	Cloths Foot	Yards Deep	Reef-Bands	Leech-Linings	Buntlings	Gores	Reef-Tackle Pieces	Clue-Pieces	Sort of Canvas	Total Yards
Sprit-Course	18	18	5⅓	....	....	....	....	....	....	3	96
Top-Sail	11	18	6¼	....	....	....	....	....	....	7	97
Flying-Jib	....	10	12	....	....	....	7	....	2	8	69
Jib	....	17	16	....	....	....	10¼	....	3	7	149¼
Fore-Course	24½	23¼	9¼	9¼	20½	12½	4	....	....	1	268⁷⁄₁₂
Foot-Band	....	....	....	....	....	....	....	....	....	2	6
Middle do.	....	....	....	....	....	....	....	....	....	2	7
Top-Sail	15¼	25	11¾	23	24½	7½	....	5	....	3	292¹¹⁄₁₂
Foot-Band	....	....	....	....	....	....	....	....	....	4	5¼
Middle do.	....	....	....	....	....	....	....	....	....	4	7
Top-Lining	....	....	....	....	....	....	....	....	....	6	25½
Top-Gallant-Sail	11	16½	6¾	....	....	....	....	....	....	7	86
Royal	7½	12	4½	....	....	....	....	....	....	8	43⁷⁄₈
Main-Course	28	30	10	10¼	22½	13⅓	6	....	....	1	342¼
Foot-Band	....	....	....	....	....	....	....	....	....	2	8
Middle do.	....	....	....	....	....	....	....	....	....	2	9
Top-Sail	18	28½	12¾	26	26½	8	....	5	....	3	353¹¹⁄₁₂
Foot-Band	....	....	....	....	....	....	....	....	....	4	6
Middle do.	....	....	....	....	....	....	....	....	....	4	7½
Top-Lining	....	....	....	....	....	....	....	....	....	6	31⅓
Top-Gallant-Sail	12½	18	6¾	....	....	....	....	....	....	7	104⅜
Royal	8	13	5	....	....	....	....	....	....	8	52½
Mizen-Course	9½	10½	8½ 15	2	....	....	6	....	6	3	130½
Top-Sail	12	18	7½ 8½	12⅝	18	6⅓	4	....	2½	5	155⅝
Foot-Band	....	....	....	....	....	....	....	....	....	6	3½
Middle do.	....	....	....	....	....	....	....	....	....	6	4½
Top-Lining	....	....	....	....	....	....	....	....	....	7	13¾
Top-Gallant-Sail	8	13	3¾ 4½	....	....	....	2½	....	....	8	41⅝
Royal	5	8½	3½	....	....	....	....	....	....	8	22
Stay-Sails, Fore	....	13	9¼	5½	....	....	....	....	2	2	67¾
Fore-Top	....	12	11¾	....	....	....	....	....	2	6	72½
Main	....	19	10	8	....	....	....	....	2	2	105
Main-Top	15	17	6 16	....	....	....	....	....	6	6	177
Main-Top-Gallant	12	12	2½ 9½	....	....	....	....	....	4½	7	76½
Royal	8	8	3 6½	....	....	....	....	....	4½	8	42½
Middle	13	13	4 10	....	....	....	....	....	5	7	96
Mizen	12	13	5 9	....	....	....	....	....	5½	3	92
Mizen-Top	9	10	3 9½	....	....	....	....	....	4½	7	62½
Studding-Sails, Fore	10	10	10¾	....	....	....	....	....	....	7	107½
Fore-Top	7	10	12½	....	....	....	....	....	....	7	106½
Fore-Top-Gallant	5	7	6¾	....	....	....	....	....	....	8	40¼
Main	11	11	11¾	2	....	....	....	....	....	7	151½
Main-Top	8	11	13½	1½	....	....	....	....	....	7	129½
Main-Top-Gallant	6	8	7¼	....	....	....	....	....	....	8	56⅝
Driver	14½	19	8 14¾	....	....	....	20	....	5	5	218½
Try-Sail	4½	8	8 9¼	6½	....	....	6¾	....	10½	1	79⁷⁄₁₂

T

DIMENSIONS OF THE SAILS, AND QUANTITY OF CANVAS

Contained in every Part of each Sail, with the Sorts of Canvas of which they are respectively made, for

A SLOOP OF 361 TONS.

NAMES OF THE SAILS.	Cloths: Head	Cloths: Foot	Yards Deep	Reef-Bands	Leech-Linings	Buntlings	Gores	Reef-Tackle Pieces	Clue-Pieces	Sort of Canvas	Total Yards
Sprit-Course	17	17	5							4	85
Top-Sail	10½	17½	6							7	84
Flying Jib		9	11¼				6¾		2	8	59¾
Jib		16	15				9¼		3	7	132¼
Fore-Course	24	23	8¾	9⅔	18⅔	11⅔	4			1	249⅝
Foot-Band										2	6
Middle do.										2	6¾
Top-Sail	15½	24½	10¾	22½	22¼	6¾		2½		4	263¼
Foot-Band										5	5⅛
Middle do.										5	6½
Top-Lining										7	23½
Top-Gallant-Sail	10½	16	5⅓							7	70⅔
Royal	6½	11	4							8	35
Main-Course	27	29	9⅓	11	21	12½	6			1	311⅚
Foot-Band										2	7⅔
Middle do.										2	8⅔
Top-Sail	17	28	12	25½	25	7⅓		2½		4	327⅙
Foot-Band										5	6
Middle do.										5	7¼
Top-Lining										7	29½
Top-Gallant-Sail	12	18	6							7	90
Royal	7½	12½	4⅓							8	43⅓
Mizen-Course	9	9½	7¾ 14	1¾			5		6	4	112⅓
Top-Sail	12	18	7¾ 8½	12⅝	18	5⅓	4		2½	6	155 5/12
Foot-Band										7	3½
Middle do.										7	4½
Top-Lining										7	13⅜
Top-Gallant-Sail	8	12½	3¾ 4¼				2¼			8	40⅜
Royal	5	8½	3¼							8	21 11/12
Stay-Sails, Fore		13	8¾	5½					2	3	64⅜
Fore-Top		12	10¾						2	6	66½
Main		18	9⅓	7⅔					2	3	93⅜
Main-Top	15	17	6 16						6	6	177
Main-Top-Gallant	12	12	2½ 9½						4½	7	76½
Royal	8	8	2¾ 6¼						4½	8	40½
Middle	13	13	4 10						5	7	96
Mizen	12	13	5 9						5½	4	92
Mizen-Top	9	10	3 9½						4½	7	62½
Studding-Sails, Fore	10	10	10¼							7	102½
Fore-Top	7	10	11½							7	97¾
Fore-Top-Gallant	5	7	5¾							8	34½
Main	11	11	11	1¾						7	122¾
Main-Top	8	11	12¾							7	122⅝
Main-Top-Gallant	6	8	6½							8	45½
Driver	14	19	7½ 14				19		5	5	202⅜
Try-Sail	5½	7	9¼ 8¼	5			5½		9	1	60¼

DIMENSIONS OF THE SAILS, AND QUANTITY OF CANVAS

Contained in every Part of each Sail, with the Sorts of Canvas of which they are respectively made, for

A BRIG OF 14 GUNS, OR 200 TONS.

NAMES OF THE SAILS.	Cloths		Yards Deep	Reef-Bands	Leech-Linings	Buntlings	Gores	Reef-Tackle Pieces	Clue and Peek Pieces	Sort of Canvas	Total Yards
	Head	Foot									
Jib	....	12	13	....	....	....	8	....	3	7	89
Sprit-Sail-Course	15	15	4	6½	....	....	....	....	....	4	66½
Top-Sail	10½	15½	6	....	....	....	....	....	....	8	78
Fore-Stay-Sail	....	9	9	....	....	....	....	....	3	4	43½
Top-Stay-Sail	....	10	10	....	....	....	....	....	3	6	53
Course	19	18	7½	7	16½	7½	23¼	....	....	2	193
Middle-Bands	....	....	....	....	....	....	....	....	....	7	11½
Top-Sail	13	19½	9½	9⅝	20	9½	2⅝	2	....	....	198⅞
Middle-Bands	....	....	....	....	....	....	....	....	....	7	10½
Top-Lining	....	....	....	....	....	....	....	....	....	7	16
Top-Gallant-Sail	10½	14	5½	....	....	....	....	....	1½	8	72
Royal	7½	11	4	....	....	....	....	....	....	8	37
Studding-Sail	10	10	9	....	....	....	....	....	1	7	91
Top-Studding-Sail	8	10	10¼	....	....	....	....	....	....	7	184½
Top-Gallant do.	6	8	6¼	....	....	....	....	....	....	8	43¾
Main-Sail	12½	19½	13 8¾	21	8¾	....	3½	....	6	1	213¼
Top-Sail	13	19½	9¾	9½	20½	11	2¾	2	....	4	214
Top-Lining	....	....	....	....	....	....	....	....	....	7	15
Top-Gallant-Sail	10½	14	5½	....	....	....	....	....	2½	8	73
Royal	7½	11	4	....	....	....	....	....	....	8	37
Stay-Sail	13	14	9 1	....	....	....	..	....	2½	2	70
Top-Stay-Sail	12	13	11 5	....	....	2½	....	....	3	6	111¾
Top-Studding-Sail	8	10	10½	1½	....	....	....	....	....	7	96
Top-Gallant do.	6	8	6¼	....	....	....	....	....	....	8	43
Ring-Tail-Sail	5½	9	16½ 14	....	....	....	14	....	....	8	122¾

DIMENSIONS OF THE SAILS, AND QUANTITY OF CANVAS

Contained in every Part of each Sail, with the Sorts of Canvas of which they are respectively made, for

A CUTTER OF 14 GUNS, OR 200 TONS, AND BOATS OF ABOUT 6 TONS.

NAMES OF THE SAILS.	Cloths		Yards Deep	Reef-Bands	Leech-Linings	Buntlings	Gores	Reef-Tackle Pieces	Clue and Peek Pieces	Sort of Canvas	Total Yards
	Head	Foot									
First Jib	1	22	20		6		66			8	302
Second Jib	1	20	19		6		64			6	269½
Third Jib	1	16	16		6		38			3	180
Fourth Jib	1	10	10		6		24			1	85
Storm Jib	1	8	8		6		14			1	56
Top-Sail	23	27	15¼ 13¾	10					6	7	378
Top-Lining										8	14
Top-Gallant-Sail	7	17	6½							8	78
Cross-Jack	30	30	20							6	600
Ring-Tail-Sail	6	12	27 24							7	225
Water-Sail	5	5	15							6	45
Main Studding-Sail	10	13	20		2					7	232
Top-Studding-Sail	8	12	15	1½						8	151½
Top-Gallant do.	5	8	7							8	45½
Fore-Sail	1	16	20½ 16		8		21			8	186½
Storm-Fore-Sail	1	15	12		8		17			2	121
Try-Sail	9	19	17½ 14	8½	14		35		6½	1	284½
Strengthening-Bands										1	24
Main-Sail	24	34	24 18		18		45		10	1	682
BOATS' SAILS.											
Latteen-Sail		7	6¼							7	21⅞
Settee-Sail	10	11	7 1							7	42
Lug-Sail	5	7	5 3¼							7	24¾
Sprit-Sails, Main	5½	6½	7¼ 5¼							7	37½
Fore	4½	5½	6 4¾							7	27
Mizen	3	3	3¼ 2¾							7	9¾
Jib		3	4½							8	6¾
Fore-Sail		3	5							8	7½

NUMBER OF SAILS IN A SUIT FOR EIGHT MONTHS' SERVICE IN THE ROYAL NAVY.

2 Main-Courses	1 Main-Top-Gallant-Stay-Sail
2 Main-Top-Sails	1 Fore-Top-Mast-Stay-Sail
1 Main-Top-Gallant-Sail	2 Jibs
1 Main-Royal	1 Flying-Jib
2 Fore-Courses	1 Mizen-Top-Mast-Stay-Sail
2 Fore-Top-Sails	1 Mizen-Royal-Stay-Sail
2 Fore-Top-Gallant-Sails	2 Main-Studding-Sails
1 Fore-Royal	2 Main-Top-Mast-Studding-Sails
2 Mizen-Courses	2 Main-Top-Gallant-Studding-Sails
2 Mizen-Top-Sails	2 Fore-Studding-Sails
1 Mizen-Top-Gallant-Sail	2 Fore-Top-Mast-Studding Sails
1 Mizen Royal	1 Fore-Top-Gallant-Studding-Sail
1 Main-Stay-Sail	1 Sprit-Sail-Course
2 Fore-Stay-Sails	1 Sprit-Sail-Top-Sail
1 Mizen-Stay-Sail	1 Driver or Spanker-Boom-Sail
2 Main-Top-Mast-Stay-Sails	1 Smoke-Sail
1 Middle-Stay-Sail	1 Royal-Stay-Sail

THE QUALITY OF CANVAS OF WHICH THE DIFFERENT SAILS ARE MADE IN THE MERCHANT-SERVICE.

CANVAS OF No. 1.

Main and Fore-Courses, and Main and Fore-Stay-Sails, of East India Ships.

CANVAS OF No. 2.

Main and Fore-Stay-Sails, and Main and Fore-Courses, of West India Ships.

CANVAS OF No. 3.

Main and Fore-Top-Sails, Mizen-Courses, Mizen-Stay-Sails, and Sprit-Sail-Courses, of large East India Ships.

CANVAS OF No. 4.

Mizen-Top-Sails of East India Ships.

CANVAS OF No. 5.

Mizen-Top-Sails of West India Ships, Main-Top-Mast-Stay-Sails of East India Ships, and Driver or Spanker Boom-Sails of large East India Ships.

CANVAS OF No. 6.

Fore-Top-Mast-Stay-Sails of East India Ships, Main-Top-Mast-Stay-Sails of West India Ships, and Driver or Spanker Boom-Sails of East and West India Ships, Sprit-Sail-Top-Sails, and Main and Fore-Top-Gallant-Sails of large East India Ships.

CANVAS OF No. 7.

Main and Fore-Top-Gallant-Sails, Middle-Stay-Sails, Flying-Jibs, Lower-Studding-Sails, Main-Top-Mast-Studding-Sails, Main-Top-Gallant-Stay-Sail of East and West India Ships, and Fore-Top-Mast-Stay-Sail of West India Ships.

CANVAS OF No. 8.

Small Flying-Jibs in large East India Ships, Mizen-Top-Gallant-Sails, and Main-Top Gallant-Studding-Sails of East and West India Ships, Mizen-Top-Mast-Stay-Sails of East India Ships, and Royals, if any.

A TABLE of the QUANTITY of CANVAS and other MATERIALS used in making a SUIT of SAILS for a Ship of each Rate, for Eight Months' Service in the Royal Navy, and a Single Suit of Sails for East and West India Ships.

When a Suit of Sails is made of the best Canvas, with the best Materials, and estimated, when finished, one with another, at Two Shillings and Twopence each Yard, the Value will be obtained as nearly as possible. But single Sails vary in Price according to the Quality of Canvas, &c. Main, Fore, Mizen, and Sprit-Courses, Top-Sails, and Stay-Sails, are sewed with Twine waxed by Hand with genuine Bees-Wax, mixed with One-Sixth Part of clear Turpentine. The other small Sails are sewed with Twine, which, and also the ordinary or roping Twine, is to be dipped in a Composition of Bees-Wax 4lb., Hog's Lard 5lb., and clear Turpentine 1lb., for the Royal Navy, and Tar only, in the Merchant-Service. Charcoal and Hog's-Lard are now seldom used, the first being substituted by Sawdust, and the latter by Tallow.

Quantity and Quality of Canvas, with the Price per Yard, and the Pounds Weight of each Bolt of Canvas, 38 Yards to the Bolt. 1821.
N. B. *All the principal Sails, at least those made of Canvas No. 1, 2, and 3, should be of Coker.*

	No. 1.	No. 2.	No. 3.	No. 4.	No. 5.	No. 6.	No. 7.	No. 8.	Total No. of Yards.
Coker····	2s. 0d.	1s 11d	1s 10d	1s. 9d.	1s. 8d.	1s. 7d.	1s. 6d.	1s. 5d.	
Com. Scotch	1s. 6d.	1s 5½d	1s. 5d.	1s 4½d	1s. 4d.	1s 3½d	1s. 3d.	1s 2½d	
	44 ℔	41 ℔	38 ℔	35 ℔	32 ℔	29 ℔	24 ℔	21 ℔	
Guns.	Yards.	Yards.	Yards.	Yards.	Yards.	Yards.	Yards.	Yards.	Yards.
3 Decks 100	3509¼	4320½	88⅓	879	1958¾	5180	1074	394½	17404
3 Decks 90	3169	4188	87	824	1823	4705	969	357	16122
2 Decks 80	4080¼	4759	91⅓	909	2040½	4990½	1036	400⅝	18316½
2 Decks 74	3659½	4327	86	862½	1892½	4881⅔	986	359½	17054⅔
2 Decks 64	3023½	3576½	79¼	695	1528½	3891	756	289⅝	13839⅛
2 Decks 50	2544	3036½	72½	596	1373	3262 10/12	641¼	251¾	11777 10/12
Frigates 60	3023 7/12	3571½	80	702½	1528½	3890½	755¾	289 10/12	13841¼
Frigates 46	2323 7/12	481	3058⅔	73½	1062	933	3153⅛	845	11930 1/12
Frigates 36	2231½	483⅝	2847	72	1001¾	921⅙	3105⅛	710⅜	11372 7/12
Frigates 32	1954¼	431⅛	2523	64 10/12	875 7/12	855	2881	604⅝	10189⅝
Frigates 28	1796⅞	409 11/12	2331⅓	61 5/12	805 5/12	834 10/12	2233⅓	539⅝	9012½
Frigates 24	1447½	337 1/12	2006 10/12	57	656 5/12	673⅔	2220½	481 1/12	7879⅔
Frigates 20	1376 11/12	325	1864 5/12	54⅞	626¾	663 11/12	2083⅙	434	7428⅓
Sloops 422T.	1301 7/12	300¼	1742⅙	51½	529 7/12	555 10/12	1923 1/12	425½	6829½
Sloops 361 "	1183⅙	55 10/12	222 5/12	1582½	252⅙	731⅓	1854 11/12	366⅔	6249 1/12
E. I. 1200 "	1373	····	1788	306	744	835	1331	496	6873
E. I. 700 "	952½	·····	1291	262	270	436	1384½	285½	4881½
W. I. 500 "	·····	582½	714	·····	151½	262¼	1010½	130	2851
W. I. 400 "	·····	446	615	·····	156	297	847½	156	2517½

Guns.	Old Canvas.	Twine. Extra, or Fine.	Twine. Ord. or Great.	Lines. Hambro'.	Lines. Log.	Bees-Wax.	Rosin.	Turpentine.	Tallow.	Oil, Train.	Tar.	Spunyarn.	Yards of sewing with Twine waxed.	Yards of sewing with Twine dipped	Bolt Rope. cwt	Bolt Rope. qr.	Bolt Rope. ℔
	Y.	℔	℔	No.	No.	℔	℔	℔	℔	Gal.	Bur.	Cwt.			cwt	qr.	℔
3 Decks 100	103	366	178	45	23	59	53	16	125	41	7	6	51778	31624	33	2	24
3 Decks 90	96	320	165	43	21	56	51	14	122	38	6	5½	42132	26517	31	0	14
2 Decks 80	106	375	196	47	25	60	45	17	127	42	8	6½	54850	35321	35	1	9
2 Decks 74	100	360	174	44	22	58	52	14	123	40	7	6	51314	30572	33	0	7
2 Decks 64	77	280	160	40	19	48	45	12	114	30	5	5	38972	17879	24	3	9
2 Decks 50	72	235	127	37	17	42	38	10	102	25	4	4	34683	15627	17	2	14
Frigates 60	77	281	165	40	19	48	45	12	90	30	5	5	38652	17984	24	3	9
Frigates 46	70	235	130	37	17	43	40	10	103	26	4½	4	35742	15972	17	3	24
Frigates 36	68	232	127	36	16	42	39	9	88	23	4	3¾	33531	14979	16	3	21
Frigates 32	62	230	120	33	14	39	34	9	85	20	3½	3	32173	15547	16	0	18
Frigates 28	57	219	115	31	13	35	31	8	78	17	3	2¾	25425	12098	14	2	14
Frigates 24	50	175	101	30	12	30	25	7	74	14	2½	2¼	24485	11872	12	2	0
Frigates 20	48	167	98	30	10	28	24	7	66	13	2	2	22475	10919	12	0	7
Sloops 422T.	45	145	79	25	9	26	23	6	62	12	2	1¾	21485	10134	9	3	6
Sloops 361 "	42	135	70	23	8	25	21	6	56	10	1¾	1⅓	19724	9693	9	0	0
E. I. 1200 "	45	145	96	22	7	26	23	3	35	3	2	2	31619	Tarred only.	9	3	21
E. I. 700 "	36	117	69	20	5	20	16	2	28	3	1¾	1¾	19955	Tarred only.	6	1	0
W. I. 500 "	19	70	40	16	4	11	9	1½	16	2	1½	1½	12907	Tarred only.	3	3	7
W. I. 400 "	16	63	35	11	3	10	7	1	13	1½	1	1	12314	Tarred only.	2	3	27

PARLIAMENTARY REGULATIONS

RELATIVE TO

SAILS AND SAIL-CLOTH.

The manufacturing of sails and sail-cloth has attracted the attention of the legislature. Regulations have been established and encouragements given, from time to time, for the maker of sail-cloth as well as for the sail-maker.

The act of the 7 and 8 William III. c. 10, § 14, enacts, "That so much of English sail-cloth as shall be found fit for the service of his Majesty's navy, shall have the preference of all foreign sail-cloth; and the commisssioners of the navy are directed and required, from time to time, to contract and agree for such English-made sail-cloth, and to allow the makers and manufacturers thereof a recompence of two-pence per yard for the same, above what they pay for foreign cloth of equal strength and goodness."

The acts, however, that materially affect this subject, are the 9 Geo. II. c. 37, and the 19 Geo. II. c. 27, both of which, though originally made to continue for seven years only, were found so beneficial, that they were rendered perpetual (except provisions relating to duties), by the 45 Geo. III. c. 68; the latter remains still in force, but part of the former has been lately repealed by 1 Geo. IV. c. 25, that is, as much "as relates to the materials to be used in the manufacture of *British* sail-cloth, and the manner of manufacturing the same." We here subjoin correct abstracts of both.

Abstract of "An Act for further encouraging and regulating the manufacture of British sail-cloth, and for the more effectual securing the duties* now payable on foreign sail-cloth imported into this kingdom."

All foreign-made sail-cloth or canvas, usually entered as hollands, duck, or vitry canvas, fit for the making of sails, and imported into Great Britain by way of merchandize, for which any

---

* The Duties are now reduced by the Tariff of July, 1842.

duties are payable, shall be stamped at the time of the landing thereof, in the port where the same shall be imported or landed.

The commissioners of the customs shall provide stamps for all foreign-made sail-cloth or canvas imported, with which, after the duty is paid, it shall be stamped; and for that purpose the commissioners shall cause stamps to be distrtbuted to the proper officers of the customs, at every port where such foreign-made sail-cloth or canvas shall be imported; which officers are required to stamp every such piece or parcel of foreign-made sail-cloth or canvas: the stamp shall denote the place or country from whence the said cloth or canvas shall be imported; and the commissioners, in providing the stamps, shall take care that they be so contrived that the impression may be durable, and so as the same may be the least liable to be counterfeited; and the said stamps may be altered or renewed, from time to time, as his Majesty shall think fit; and if any person shall counterfeit or forge any such stamp or impression upon any foreign-made sail-cloth, then such person so offending, and duly convicted thereof, shall forfeit the sum of fifty pounds; and if any person shall sell, or expose to sale, any such foreign-made sail-cloth with a counterfeit stamp thereon, knowing the same to be counterfeit, such offender shall forfeit the sum of fifty pounds.

And for the better ascertaining and distinguishing the sail-cloth of the British manufacture from foreign sail-cloth, every manufacturer of sail-cloth in Great Britain shall affix or impress, or cause to be fixed or impressed, on every piece of sail-cloth by him manufactured, a stamp, containing the name and place of abode of such manufacturer, in plain distinct letters, and words at length; and if any manufacturer of sail-cloth, or other person, shall sell or expose to sale, or work up into sails, any piece or bolt of British sail-cloth without being stamped as aforesaid, such manufacturer or other person so offending, and being thereof lawfully convicted upon the oath of one or more credible witness or witnesses, before any justice of the peace for the place where the offence shall be committed, shall forfeit the sum of ten pounds for every piece of sail-cloth by him or them sold or exposed to sale, or worked up into sails, not being so stamped; and if any person shall wilfully or maliciously cut off, destroy, or obliterate, any stamp so affixed (except in the tarring or working up the same), or shall affix or impress any stamp on which shall be stamped the name or place of abode of any other person, and not his or their real name or names and place or places of abode, such person, being convicted of any of the said offences, shall, for every offence, forfeit the sum of five pounds; which last-mentioned forfeiture shall be levied and recovered by distress and sale of the offender's goods and chattels, by warrant under the hands and seals of two or more justices of the peace for the place where the offence shall be committed, and shall be applied to the use of the informer or informers.

And, for encouraging the use and consumption of the manufacture of British sail-cloth, every ship or vessel which shall be built in Great Britain, and every ship or vessel which shall be built in any of his Majesty's plantations in America, shall, upon her first setting out to sea, have or be furnished with one full and complete set of sails, made up of sail-cloth manufactured in Great Britain; and in case such ship shall not, on her first setting out, be so fitted out and furnished, that then, and for every such neglect and default, the master of such ship shall forfeit the sum of fifty pounds.

No sail-maker, or other person, in this kingdom, shall make up into sails or tarpawlins any foreign-made sail-cloth or canvas, not stamped according to the directions of this act; and in case any person shall make or work up into sails or tarpawlins any foreign-made sail-cloth or canvas, other than as aforesaid, such sails and tarpawlins shall be forfeited; and such sail-maker, &c. shall likewise forfeit the sum of twenty pounds.

All sail-cloth made in Great Britain shall be manufactured in the manner and according to the directions hereinafter mentioned, viz. every piece or bolt of British sail-cloth, that shall be 24 inches in breadth, and 38 yards in length, shall weigh according to the numbers and weights here mentioned, viz. No. 1, 44 pounds each bolt; No. 2, 41; No. 3, 38; No. 4, 35; No. 5, 32; No. 6, 29; No. 7, 24; No. 8, 21; No. 9, 18; and No. 10, 15 pounds each bolt.

And in case any piece or bolt of either of such respective numbers or sorts of British sail-cloth shall be made of a different breadth or length than before-mentioned, such piece or bolt of British sail-cloth shall be increased or diminished in weight, in proportion to the difference in such length or breadth, and shall be marked or stamped with such number as shall be agreeable to the weight; and the warp or chain of every piece or bolt of the first six numbers of such British sail-cloth shall be wholly wrought and made of double yarn, and shall contain, in every piece or bolt of 24 inches in breadth, at least 560 double threads of yarn; and in every piece of such sail-cloth, that shall be 30 inches in breadth, at least 700 double threads of yarn; and in every bolt of such sail-cloth, that shall be of any other breadths than as aforesaid, a certain number or quantity of double threads of yarn, in proportion to the number of double threads of yarn expressed to be contained in the breadth, as aforesaid, and the warp and shoot-yarn, which shall be wrought in every piece or bolt of the first four numbers of such sail-cloth, shall be made of long flax, without any mixture of short or bar flax, or of long flax, or Italian hemp, or Braak hemp; and all the flax and hemp used in making the warp and shoot-yarn of such sail-cloth, of the aforesaid first four numbers, shall be of a strong staple, fresh, sound, and good in its kind, and well dressed; and the yarn well cleansed, even spun, and well twisted; and all the shoot-yarn of each piece of sail-cloth of the first four numbers shall be full as strong as the warp-yarn, and close stuck with four shoots of treble threads, at the distance of every two feet or thereabouts; and both the warp and shoot-yarn shall be as strong as the warp and shoot-yarn that are usually wrought in the sail-cloth of those first four numbers that are made for and used in his Majesty's navy; and no flax-yarn used in any British sail-cloth shall be whitened with lime, on forfeiture of sixpence per yard for every yard that shall be so whitened, made, sold, or worked up into new sails, in Great Britain, any ways essentially different, lighter, or inferior in strength and goodness, to any of the aforesaid directions or restrictions.

Every sail-maker or other person, who shall make or work up sail-cloth into sails or tarpawlins, shall cause this act, or an abstract thereof, to be put up or affixed, there to continue, in some public part of the loft, shop, or workshop, where his said trade is carried on, or his workmen employed, under the penalty of forty shillings.

Abstract of "An Act for the more effectual securing the duties now payable on foreign-made sail-cloth imported into this kingdom; for charging all foreign-made sails with a duty; and for explaining a doubt concerning ships being obliged at their first setting out to sea to be furnished with one complete set of sails made of British sail-cloth."

Every master of any ship or vessel belonging to any of his Majesty's subjects, navigated with any foreign-made sail or sails, or who shall have any foreign-made sail or sails on board his ship or vessel, shall, at the time of making his entry or report of such ship or vessel at the Custom-house, make a report upon oath of all foreign-made sails used in or being on board such ship or vessel; and he shall, before such ship or vessel is cleared by the officers of the customs inwards, where such ship makes any discharge of her lading, pay the same duties as are payable for all foreign-made sails imported by way of merchandize.*

Every such sail shall be stamped at the port where such ship makes her entry, in manner hereinafter mentioned; and in case the master of such ship shall not make the said entry, and pay such duty before the ship shall be cleared by the officers of the customs, such sails shall be forfeited, and the master shall for every offence forfeit the sum of fifty pounds, one moiety thereof to the use of his Majesty, and the other moiety to the person who shall sue for the same.

Provided always, if the master of such ship shall, after his report made, and before the ship is cleared by the officers of the customs, declare his intention of not paying the said duty, and shall deliver to the officers of the customs of the port where he makes such report, the sails for which he has declared his intention of not paying the said duty; in such case the sails are hereby declared to be forfeited to his Majesty; and such master shall not be subject or liable to pay the said duty or penalty of fifty pounds.

Provided always, that nothing herein contained shall be deemed, construed, adjudged, or taken, to charge or make liable any captain or master of any ship coming from the East Indies, with any of the duties or forfeitures aforesaid, for or upon account of such ship being navigated with, or having on board, any foreign-made

---

* See the Duties of 1842.

sail or sails, which shall be by such captain or master brought from the East Indies.

All foreign-made sail-cloth or canvas, usually entered as hollands, duck, or vitry canvas, fit to be made use of for the making of sails, which shall be imported into Great Britain, by way of merchandize, and upon the importation whereof any duties are made payable, shall be stamped at the time of the landing thereof, at or in the port or place where the same shall be imported, as hereafter mentioned.

And whereas the stamps used in pursuance of the former act are of too small dimensions, and make a very obscure mark and impression, liable to be soon defaced and become undistinguishable, it is enacted, that the commissioners of the customs shall provide stamps of eight inches diameter each, for the stamping of all foreign-made sails and foreign-made sail-cloth, and shall cause the said stamps to be distributed amongst proper officers of the customs, of every port in Great Britain; and the officers of every port are hereby required to stamp all foreign-made sails, and foreign-made sail-cloth, which shall be imported into the several ports where they reside; and which stamps shall, in order to make the impression durable, be dipped in a liquor made of red-lead, mixed with linseed-oil well boiled; and the stamp or impression therewith made shall express and denote the place and port in which such sails and foreign-made sail-cloth are entered; and the commissioners, in providing the stamps, shall take care that they be so contrived, that the impression may be plain and durable, and so as the same may be the least liable to be counterfeited; and if any person shall counterfeit or forge any stamp provided in pursuance of this act, upon any foreign-made sail-cloth, or foreign-made sails, or shall sell such sail-cloth with counterfeited or forged stamps, knowing the same to be forged, then such person so offending shall forfeit the sum of fifty pounds.

No sail-maker or other person, within Great Britain or in his Majesty's plantations in America, shall make up into sails or tarpawlins any foreign-made sail-cloth not stamped according to this act; and in case any person shall make up into sails or tarpawlins any foreign sail-cloth other than as aforesaid, such sails and tarpawlins shall be forfeited; and every person so offending, and being thereof lawfully convicted, upon the oath of one or more credible witnesses, before one or more justices of the peace for the place where the offence shall be committed, shall forfeit the sum of fifty pounds for every such sail or tarpawlin: which penalty of fifty pounds shall be levied and recovered by distress and sale of the offender's goods and chattels, by warrant under the hands and seals of two or more justices of the peace for the place where the offence shall be committed, and shall go and be applied to the use of the informers; and for want of such distress, such justices may commit such person to gaol for the space of six months, or until he pays the penalty of fifty pounds.

Every person who shall make up into sails any foreign-made sail-cloth, shall place the stamps affixed or impressed on such foreign sail-cloth in the most conspicuous part of such sails, that is to say, on the aft-side of such sails, and in such manner, that the number of stamps in every sail may appear proportionably to the number of bolts or pieces contained in the said sail; and in case any person shall make up any foreign-made sail-cloth or canvas, into sails, in any other manner than as aforesaid, such sails shall be forfeited, and such person shall for every offence forfeit the sum of ten pounds.

No person whatsoever shall alter, repair, or mend, any sails, made of foreign-made sail-cloth, not stamped according to this act; and in case any person shall alter, repair, or mend, any sails not stamped as aforesaid, such person shall, for every sail so mended, forfeit the sum of twenty pounds.

Every sail-maker in Great Britain, and in his Majesty's plantations in America, shall affix or impress, or cause to be affixed or impressed, on every new sail by him so made, a stamp, eight inches in diameter, containing the name and place of abode of such sail-maker, in plain distinct letters, and words at length; and which said stamp, in order to make the impression durable, shall be dipped in a liquid made with lamp-black, mixed with linseed-oil well boiled; and in case any person shall make any new sail, and shall deliver the same to any captain or master of any ship or vessel, not being stamped with his name and place of abode, such sail shall be forfeited; and every person shall, for every sail by him so delivered, not stamped, forfeit the sum of ten pounds.

And whereas doubts have arisen about the meaning of a clause in the preceding act, of the ninth year of his present Majesty's reign, by which ships are obliged, at their first setting out, or being first navigated at sea, to be furnished with one full and complete set of sails, made of sail-cloth manufactured in Great Britain: to obviate such doubts for the future, it is enacted, that every ship or vessel built in Great Britain, or in his Majesty's plantations in America, shall, upon her first setting out, or being first navigated, be furnished with one complete set of new sails, (*bonâ fide* belonging to such ship or vessel,) made of sail-cloth manufactured in Great Britain; and in case such ship or vessel shall not, on her first setting out, be furnished with a new set of sails, made of sail-cloth of the manufacture of Great Britain, as aforesaid, that, for every such default, the master of such ship or vessel shall forfeit the sum of fifty pounds.

It has been subsequently enacted, by the 33 Geo. III. c. 49, that no part of the penalties contained in the 9 Geo. II. c. 37, which do not attach to double sail-cloth, shall extend to British canvas, made with single-thread warps, corded or not corded, and fit for, or made into sails. And that such single canvas shall be deemed British sail-cloth, and be equally entitled, with double canvas, to the bounties. Provided that the said single-thread sail-cloth be made of equally good materials, and be conformable, in weight and all other things, to the restrictions on double-thread sail-cloth.

It is the practice of Government to mark each bolt or piece of canvas, before it is made up into sails, with a blue streak down the middle; made with a composition of linseed-oil, white-lead, and ground indigo, well boiled together.

By the 9 and 10 Wm. III. c. 41, any person in whose possession any canvas with the blue streak up the middle, being the king's mark, is found, without a certificate of its having been purchased of the commissioners of the navy, forfeits the property, and is liable to the penalty of two hundred pounds, with costs of suit. By the 9 Geo. I. c. 8. the judge, before whom such offender is convicted, is empowered to mitigate the penalty, commit until the same be paid; or kept to hard labour for a time, not exceeding six months.

The commissioners of his Majesty's navy, by the 1 Geo. I. c. 15, are empowered, for embezzlement of the king's stores, under the value of twenty shillings, to fine the offender, not exceeding double the value taken; or to imprison, not exceeding three months.

Sails and Cordage of British manufacture, exported from Great Britain to the colonies, and afterwards imported into the United Kingdom, are in all cases, other than those in which they are imported by *bill of store*, to be deemed foreign; and such Sails and Cordage, although not liable to duty so long as the vessel continues to belong to the colony, become subject to the duties in question as soon as the vessel becomes the property of persons residing in this country.—(*Treasury Order, 29th January,* 1828.)

DUTIES PAYABLE UPON THE IMPORTATION OF SAIL-CLOTH AND SAILS,

ACCORDING TO THE TARIFF OF JULY, 1842.

	Of or from Foreign Countries.	Of and from British Possessions.
	£ s. d.	£. s. d.
LINEN—Plain Linens and Diaper, not otherwise enumerated or described, and whether chequered or striped with dyed yarn or not, for every £100 value	15 0 0	15 0 0
———— Sails, for every £100 value	15 0 0	15 0 0
———————— in actual use of a British ship, and fit and necessary for such ship, and not otherwise disposed of	Free.	Free.
————————, if and when otherwise disposed of, for every £100 value	15 0 0	15 0 0
Thread, not otherwise enumerated or described, for every £100 value	10 0 0	5 0 0

INSTRUCTIONS

FOR

MANUFACTURING CANVAS FOR HER MAJESTY'S NAVY.

Admiralty, April, 1842.

FIRST.

THE warp and weft of the canvas to be spun wholly from the longs of the best British or Irish, or of the best Riga, Pernau, Revel, Narva 12-head, or St. Petersburgh 12-head, or from the best long white Dutch, long white Flemish, or Friesland flax.

The flax to be free from blacks and any mixture of short flax, and to be well dressed. The yarns to be well and evenly spun, and properly twisted.

> *N.B. Although different kinds of flax are named, the Lords Commissioners of the Admiralty prefer that of British or Irish growth, but reserve to themselves the right of restricting to any one or more, as the quality or braak of flax, or other circumstances, may render necessary from time to time.*

SECOND.

Both warp and weft to be twice boiled, with best American pot and pearl ashes, and carefully and thoroughly washed and cleansed, and no acid, chloride of lime, nor other preparation of chlorine, nor any deleterious substance whatever to be used in any stage of the process.

The operations of boiling, washing, &c., to be performed as under, viz. :—

First Boil.

1. The yarns to be boiled a sufficient length of time, in a solution of the best American pot ash, in the proportion of 7 pounds ashes for every 100 pounds green yarn; the water to be in the proportion of one gallon for every pound of yarn.

2. The yarns to be mill-washed, the warp 6 minutes, and the

weft 15 minutes, then carefully washed in a considerable stream of clear running water, and wrung.

Second Boil.

1. The yarns to be again boiled for a sufficient length of time in a solution of American pearl ashes, in the proportion of 4 pounds for every 100 pounds green yarn, the water to be in the same proportion as in the first boil.

2. The yarns to be carefully rinsed or washed in a clear stream of water, and to be carefully dried, and frequently shaken in the course of drying, so that all the fibres of the flax may be equally stretched.

N.B. The yarns to be all prepared in the above manner between the 1st of February and 31st of October, and not during the months of November, December, or January.

THIRD.

No starch, tallow, paste, or weavers' dressing of any description, to be used in the manufacture of the Canvas.

FOURTH.

The warp to consist of the following proportions of clean unstarched yarn, viz.:—

No. 0 not less than 28 lbs.	16½ Score Reed,	660 Double Threads
1 26	do.	do.
2 24	do.	do.
3 22	do.	do.
4 21	17	680
5 19	do.	do.
6 18	do.	do.
7 15	20	800 Single Threads
8 14	do.	do.

FIFTH.

The Canvas to be 24 and 18 inches wide. No bolt, from No. 0 to 6 inclusive, to contain more than thirty-nine yards, and No. 7 and 8 to contain forty yards. The thrums to be left on, and the bolt of 24 inches to weigh as follows (the 18 inches in proportion), viz.

No. 0	48 pounds
1	46
2	43
3	40
4	36
5	33
6	30
7	27
8	25

SIXTH.

Each bolt to be completely manufactured, and particular attention to be paid to the weaving, so that it be struck sufficiently close. All cylindering or calendering is strictly prohibited.

SEVENTH.

The Canvas to be stamped with the manufacturer's name, place of residence, and the month and year in which it is manufactured, and the stamp to be at least three yards in the bolt. The letters to be 1 inch by $\frac{3}{4}$.

EIGHTH.

The manufactories of persons manufacturing Canvas for Her Majesty's Navy, and the works of spinners and bleachers employed by them, to be open at all times to an Inspector, or to any other person authorized by Government for the special purpose of inspecting the same.

N. B.—These Instructions are framed for the information and guidance of all Contractors, with the view of insuring the supply of Canvas of a superior quality and durability for the Navy; and any Contractor who shall deliver at any of Her Majesty's Dock Yards, Canvas made of yarns not of the description and quality specified, or not prepared in strict and full conformity to the directions contained in these Instructions, shall be held incompetent to be employed in future. And further, if any manufacturer shall, by collusion with any other person or persons part with or assign over his Contract to any other person, or introduce any other person to a share thereof, without the previous approbation of the Lords Commissioners of the Admiralty; or shall attempt to send in any other Canvas than such as has been bonâ fide manufactured by himself, in terms of, and in strict conformity to, these Instructions, his future Tender for supplying Canvas will not be accepted.

FORM OF TENDER FOR CANVAS, &c.

A Copy of these Instructions will be delivered to every manufacturer, which he is to paste on a board, and hang up in the most conspicuous place in his manufactory, for the information and guidance of all parties employed therein; and on the Day of Treaty every Tender must be accompanied by a Declaration made by the person tendering before a Magistrate, in conformity to Act 6 Wm. IV. cap. 62, that the Canvas offered by him shall, if accepted, be made entirely of Long Flax of some or one of the descriptions herein specified, prepared wholly and solely in the manner herein prescribed, and that these Instructions shall be strictly and carefully attended to in every other respect in manufacturing the same, and without such Declaration no Tender will be accepted on the Day of Treaty, and the last delivery of Canvas at each of Her Majesty's Dock Yards, in fulfilment of any Contract, must also be accompanied by a Declaration made in like manner, and particularly enumerating the said stipulations, to the effect that each and every of the same have been duly and faithfully complied with, as respects the whole of the Canvas delivered at each respective Yard under the said Contract.

FORM OF TENDER FOR CANVAS FOR HER MAJESTY'S NAVY.

Sir,

184

hereby offer to supply the following Canvas for the service of Her Majesty's Navy, viz.:

Ins.	No. of Bolts.
24 wide	_____
18 „	_____

at £   s.   d.   per cent. { advance or / abatement } on or from the undermentioned prices, namely;

Ins. 24 wide	No.	Price per Yard. d.	Ins. 18 wide	No.	Price per Yard. d.
	1	17		1	14
	2	16		2	13
	3	15		3	12
	4	14		4	11
	5	13		5	10
	6	12		6	9
	7	11		7	8½
	8	10		8	8

x 2

And   engage that the Canvas shall be made in every respect according to the "*Instructions for Manufacturing Canvas for Her Majesty's Navy,*" and to the following Conditions, and that it shall consist of such numbers, and be delivered within the time prescribed, in such proportions at Her Majesty's Dockyards at *Deptford, Portsmouth,* and *Plymouth,* as shall be determined by the Lords Commissioners of the Admiralty.

Your very humble Servant,

Signature _____

Address _____

The Secretary of the Admiralty,
   Somerset Place.

Proposed Sureties.

Christian Names at full length.	Surnames.	Place of Abode.	Profession or Business.	Names and Residence of Referee.

CONDITIONS.

Tenders may be made for any quantity not less than 1000 Bolts.

The Canvas to be delivered by the 31st of December next, and to be good, sound, merchantable, well conditioned, such as shall be approved of by the Officers of the said respective Yards, and in every respect fit for the service of Her Majesty's Navy.

Rejected Canvas to be removed by and at the expense of the Contractor, within one month after notice given to him of the rejection.

In case the Contractor fails to deliver the Canvas within the period specified, the Lords Commissioners of the Admiralty to be at liberty to purchase other Canvas in lieu thereof, and to charge him with all extra expenses.

The Contractor is to covenant not to transfer the Contract, and not to pay fees to any servant of the public in the Naval Department.

Every Tender must be accompanied by a letter, addressed to the Secretary of the Admiralty, Somerset Place, and signed by two responsible persons, offering to become bound with the person tendering, in the sum of £25 per cent. on the value of the Canvas, for the due performance of the Contract; and the said letter must contain a reference to some person or persons, well acquainted with the sufficiency of the parties so offering to become bound, and persons in partnership with the Contractor or with each other will not be accepted as Sureties.

Bills of Parcels in duplicate are to be sent to the said respective Yards by the Contractor with every delivery of Canvas. The duplicate will be returned to him by the Officers, with the quantities received by them inserted therein; and when he lodges at the Admiralty, Somerset Place, invoices thereof, claiming payment for the same (according to a form to be furnished by the Accountant-General of the Navy), bills for the amount due will immediately be made out payable at sight.

For each Yard of 36 inches legal measure, the Contractor is to deliver, according to the custom of the trade, one additional inch per Yard, without charge for the same.

Their Lordships will not treat with parties making Tenders at low prices, unless satisfied of their competency to fulfil their Contracts, both as regards the quality of Canvas required to be supplied, and the period of its delivery at Her Majesty's Dock-yards.

DECLARATION TO ACCOMPANY THE TENDER.

                                      of   in the county of   Canvas Manufacturer, do solemnly and sincerely declare, that the Canvas hereby offered by   shall, if accepted, be made entirely of long Flax, of some or one of the descriptions mentioned in the *"Instructions for Manufacturing Canvas for Her Majesty's Navy,"* prepared wholly and solely in the manner therein prescribed, and that the said Instructions shall be strictly and carefully attended to in every other respect in manufacturing the said Canvas.

    And   make this solemn Declaration, conscientiously believing the same to be true, and by virtue of the provisions of an Act made and passed in the sixth year of the reign of his late Majesty King William the Fourth, intituled "An Act to repeal an Act of the present Session of Parliament, intituled an Act for the more effectual abolition of Oaths and Affirmations taken and made in various Departments of the State, and to substitute Declarations in lieu thereof, and for the more entire Suppression of voluntary and extra-judicial Oaths and Affidavits, and to make other provisions for the abolition of unnecessary Oaths."

Declared before me at
this   day of   184

Mem°.—No Tender whatever will be accepted, unless accompanied by the above Declaration, duly subscribed and made before a Magistrate upon this printed Form.

The quantity of Canvas taken by the Government of late years, has been from 30,000 to 35,000 Bolts annually, varying from 15d. to 16½d. No. 1, falling about three farthings per yard each number from 1 to 8.

THE END.

A LIST OF VALUABLE WORKS

PUBLISHED BY

CHARLES WILSON,

(LATE J. W. NORIE AND WILSON,)

AT THE NAVIGATION WAREHOUSE AND NAVAL ACADEMY,
157, LEADENHALL STREET, LONDON.

Extracted from Catalogue, 1840.

222 *Norie's Complete Epitome of Practical Navigation,* containing all necessary Instructions for keeping a Ship's Reckoning at Sea, &c. &c. Twelfth Edition. Price 16s.

223 *Norie's* Set of *Nautical Tables.* Tenth Edition, sewed. Price 12s.

225 *Norie's* Set of *Linear Tables.* Boards. Price 15s.

227 *Norie's Seaman's new Daily Assistant.* Price 5s.

229 *Norie's* Book of *Formulæ* for finding the *Longitude* by the *Linear Tables.* Price 2s. 6d.

230 *Norie's* Book of *Formulæ* for finding the *Longitude* by the Fourth Method. Price 2s. 6d.

231 *Norie's* Book of *Formulæ* for finding the *Longitude* by *Chronometers.* Price 2s. 6d.

482 The *Shipwright's Vade Mecum;* a clear and familiar Introduction to Ship-building, including the more complex Rules of Arithmetic, made use of in that Art, with so much of the principles of practical Geometry and Mensuration as are required in the practice thereof, &c. Boards, with Four large Drafts, separately done up. Price £1. 5s.

483 The Art of making *Masts, Yards, Gaffs, Booms, Blocks,* and *Oars,* as practised in the Royal Navy, and according to the most approved Methods in the Merchant-Service, including a Description of an improved Rule for Mast-makers; also a new Method by which large Yards may be made from small Trees, and repaired when sprung in the Slings, &c. In Boards, accompanied with a separate Volume of large Engravings. Second Edition, in which is included the new Method of Douling. Price £1.

484, 485, 486 Improved *Mast Maker's Rule,* as described in the above. Price 7s. Wood Slide, 8s. Brass, and 9s. Ivory.

487 The *Art of Rigging;* containing an alphabetical Explanation of the Terms, Directions for the most minute Operations, and the Method of Progressive Rigging, with full and correct Tables of the Dimensions and Quantities of

List of Valuable Works published by Charles Wilson.

every Part of the Rigging of all Ships and Vessels, illustrated with numerous Engravings. Third Edition, considerably enlarged and improved, with additional Tables, expressly adapted for Merchant Shipping, in Boards. In the Press. Price 12s.

489 The *System of Naval Tactics;* combining the established Theory with general Practice, and particularly the late Practice of the British Navy, during the General War, and by the use of which many important Naval Battles were won. 8vo. Boards. Price 8s.

490 *Seamanship*, both in Theory and Practice, in two Parts, illustrated with numerous Engravings. 8vo. Boards. Second Edition. Price 8s. 6d.

491 The *Sea Gunner's Vade Mecum;* being an Introduction to practical Gunnery, expressly accommodated to the Use of the Royal Navy, &c. by Robert Simmons. One Volume, Boards. Price 9s.

492 *Observations and Instructions* for the Use of the Commissioned, the Junior, and other Officers of the Royal Navy, on all the material Points of professional Duty; including also Forms of general and particular Orders, for the better Government and Discipline of Her Majesty's Ships, together with a variety of new and useful Tables, by a Captain in the Royal Navy, in One Volume, 8vo. Bound. Second Edition. Price 6s.

493 *Cobin's* short and plain *Principles* of *Linear Perspective;* adapted to Naval Architecture, containing Rules to draw correctly the Forms of Ships, in every possible position, with separate Volume of Plates. Price 5s.

494 *Goodfellow's Merchant and Ship-Master's Ready Calculator.* Price 7s. 6d.

507 The *Ship-builder's Assistant* or *Marine Architecture*, revised by W. Sutherland. Price 9s.

Daniel's Charges on *Vessels* (British and Foreign) at all the Ports, Sub-ports, and Creeks of Great Britain and Ireland, and Islands thereof, comprising Pilotage, Harbour and Dock Dues, Depth of Water, Plankage, Quayage, Anchorage, Pier Lights, and Flag Fees, Buoyage, Keelage, Towage, Perches, and other Information. Cloth boards. Price 5s.

Liddel's new Seaman's Vade Mecum; containing a practical Essay on Naval Book-Keeping, with the Method of keeping the Captain's Accounts, and complete Instructions in the Duty of a Captain's Clerk, Purser, &c. in the Royal Navy. Fifth Edition, newly arranged and enlarged. Bound. Price 12s.

Steel's Atlantic and West Indian Navigator. Price 5s.

Steel's Ship Masters' Assistant and Owners' Manual, containing valuable Information necessary for Captains and Persons connected with Maritime Affairs. Price £1. 1s.

J. Dennett, Printer, 121, Fleet Street.

CPSIA information can be obtained
at www.ICGtesting.com
Printed in the USA
BVHW011744161022
649575BV00010B/367